THE LION

OF

LONDON BRIDGE

by

Roy Larner

with Dean Rinaldi

Published by Blue Mendos Publications
In association with Amazon KDP

Published in paperback 2022
Category: Life Story
Copyright Roy Larner © 2022
ISBN : 9798362597269

Cover design by Jill Rinaldi © 2022

Dedication

To my partner, Tracy Johnson and her daughter Kerry, son Shane and grandchildren Mia, Leo and Joey for your love, trust and support when I needed it most.

For my incredible mum, Phyllis, thank you for your unconditional love and to my beautiful daughter, Freya, and her mum, Tracy. My niece Demi Larner and her mum Tracy.

Not forgetting my brothers Chris, Brian and Paul. We may quarrel and annoy each other but in my heart I know that there is mutual love, care and respect.

To my friend, 'Old' Mike, who sadly passed away from cancer in 2020.

The late Costas Paphitis, thank you. I'll never forget all that you did for me.

Acknowledgements

Jill Rinaldi for creating the book cover, editor Debra Bekker and my good friend and ghostwriter, Dean Rinaldi.

I'd like to thank and acknowledge the thousands of people who have reached out from all over the world for their kind words, financial and moral support.

Eliana Caroccia

Lives in London, United Kingdom

VIEW PROFILE

20:14

 Hi Roy, apologies for this late message. I've always wanted to express my immense gratitude for your outstanding courage during the London bridge terrorist attack. Thanks to you I am still alive. You are an extraordinary persone, one of the very few on our planet. Again, thank you, and sorry for waiting so long to thank you, Eliana.

Chapter 1

Clacton-on-Sea, Essex. May 1970

"I don't understand why you had to buy post cards, we're only here a week and the cards probably won't arrive until we're back home in London," Lee said as he slipped off his shoes and pushed himself back into the arm chair.

"Its tradition," Phyllis said bluntly before turning to face the wall when she heard *'Spirit in the Sky'* by Norman Greenbaum playing on the radio in the next room

"That money would be better off in your purse. Besides, they only end up in the bin," Lee said as he rubbed his feet on the rug

"People love to receive post cards, Lee, and if you spent more time around normal people rather than the villains you associate with, you'd know that," Phyllis said as she filled the kettle.

"You don't complain when it puts food on the table and clothes on the kids back," Lee said defensively.

"You could, if you tried, just get a normal job and work nine to five and be around me and the children," Phyllis said as she lit the gas ring with a match. "It's what families do, Lee. Not everyone has to live their life in a pub with criminals, steal and then end up in prison."

"I've told you before," Lee said sharply. "I'm not a thief and I don't steal."

"Really," Phyllis said sarcastically.

"Fraud isn't stealing, well, not really," Lee said as he sat forward. "You see, taking from banks, post offices and big business isn't really like stealing. I mean, they are the biggest thieves and con men of all. Fraud isn't like breaking into some poor working guy's home and stealing his radio."

"So you see yourself like a Robin Hood, only you don't give it to the poor; just a bit for me and the kids to get by on and rest goes to the pub's landlord," Phyllis said as she poured the boiling water into a tea pot.

"I see it as morals and the law," Lee said as he leaned back and put his hands behind his head.

"Now this should be interesting," Phyllis muttered as she placed the tea strainer over one of the two cup and saucers she had placed on the worktop.

"Morals are not laws, oh no," Lee said, shaking his head emphatically. "So, everything that is illegal isn't necessarily immoral."

Phyllis poured the tea over the strainer.

"What me and a few of my mates do is okay morally, because no one is really being hurt. We're only taking some of the profits from some big faceless organisation," Lee said, looking up at the ceiling. "We all live in a world where absolutely everything is about money and it's all just one big cycle of injustice."

"And that is what stops you getting a job Lee?" Phyllis said as she handed him a cup of the freshly brewed tea.

"Well, that, and I can earn more in a few hours than I would in a month grafting for some jumped up twat in a suit that was born with a silver spoon in his mouth," Lee said before taking a sip of his tea.

Phyllis and Lee Larner had left their home in Muswell Hill, London, to holiday at a landlady run guesthouse in Clacton-on-Sea with their three children, Chris, aged 8, Brian, aged 5 and Roy who was born at the Middlesex Hospital in London's West End on the 13th of November 1969, just six months earlier. Holidaymakers from London arrived in their droves between May and September every year to escape the busy city and enjoy the seaside resort with its beach, pier and pavilion, and the beautiful gardens and pleasure boats.

Chris was reading the latest edition of the Dandy while his brother, Brian, had fallen asleep, having spent most of the day playing on the beach. Lee had bought the family chips at lunch time as the landlady had made it very clear on their arrival that no one was to return to her guesthouse before 5.00pm. Phyllis had asked what they should do if it was to rain. The landlady simply shrugged her shoulders and closed the front door behind them.

"Can you check on Roy?" Phyllis said as she filled the sink with water to wash out the children's swimwear.

"He's fast asleep," Lee said without moving from the chair.

"I asked you to check on him, please, Lee," Phyllis called out as she rinsed a pair of trunks.

Lee huffed before rocking himself forward and standing up. He walked gingerly into the adjoining bedroom where he peered down into the cot.

"He's making a bit of a funny noise," Lee called out.

Phyllis stomped into the bedroom while drying her hands. She stepped past Lee and looked down at her six month old infant.

"Arghhh!" Phyllis cried out when she saw that Roy's little face and lips had turned blue and he was gasping for air.

"What, what?" Lee yelled as he staggered back.

Phyllis reached down and took her son into her arms.

"Something is wrong with my baby," Phyllis wailed, tears streaming down her face. "We need to get to a hospital, now!"

"Right, okay, what do you want me to do?" Lee said awkwardly while watching Phyllis rock her baby back and forth.

"Come on Roy, you'll be alright," Phyllis whispered before kissing her son his head.

Phyllis looked over at Lee and yelled, "Go and get an ambulance. Now!"

Lee bolted downstairs shouting "We need an ambulance now! Now!"

The landlady grabbed the telephone and called in the emergency. With Roy in her arms, Phyllis ran down the staircase and along the hallway.

"The ambulance is on its way, Mrs Larner," the landlady said.

Phyllis held Roy in her arms and marched towards the front door.

"Open the door!"

Lee fumbled with the latch and then opened the door as an Austin Morris BMC LD ambulance raced up the road with the siren wailing and lights flashing. It came to a screeching halt outside the guesthouse. The ambulance driver scrambled out of the cab and ran around to the back to open the rear doors, while Phyllis, tears streaming down her face, strode towards the driver.

"Phyllis, what do you want me to do?" Lee called as Phyllis climbed into the back of the ambulance.

"Make sure the children are fed and washed before going to bed," Phyllis called back before the rear doors were slammed shut.

With the siren still wailing and the emergency lights flashing, the ambulance screeched away.

"Everything will be alright, Roy, stay with me, because everything will be alright," Phyllis whispered before gently kissing her son on the forehead.

The ambulance raced through the town towards the Clacton & District Hospital in Tower Road. The vehicle came to an abrupt halt and within seconds the rear doors were open and Phyllis was met by two nurses.

The older of the two nurses took Roy into her arms.

"I just looked down at him and he was blue and breathing funny," Phyllis said.

"Laboured breathing, baby's tummy is moving more than normal while breathing, and the nostrils are flared," the older nurse said.

The second nurse nodded.

"Wheezing, indicating inflammation causing breathing difficulty," the older nurse continued as she walked quickly through the emergency department.

The second nurse nodded again.

"What is the matter with my son?" Phyllis cried out as tears continued to stream down her face.

"I believe that your son may be having an asthma attack," the older nurse said. "What is your name?"

"Mrs Larner, Phyllis Larner."

"You did the right thing by getting him to hospital as quickly as you did, Mrs Larner. He is in good, safe, hands now and what I need for you to do now is to go with my colleague."

"My son! Roy needs me," Phyllis cried out as the nurse scurried away.

"My name is Nurse Walters and everything will be okay now, Mrs Larner," Nurse Walters said as she motioned Phyllis to walk with her.

"I don't understand. Where are we going?" Phyllis said, wiping the tears from her face.

"We have to do the registration process," Nurse Walters said calmly. "It's important that we do this for the patient records."

In a trance like state Phyllis provided Nurse Walters with all the required information.

"Mrs Larner, are you okay?" Nurse Walters said, reaching out and gripping her arm firmly.

"I don't want to lose my son, my Roy," Phyllis sobbed.

Phyllis began to rock back and forth. Nurse Walters tightened her grip.

"Mrs Larner, do you feel okay?"

Phyllis began to hyperventilate. She put her hand over her pounding heart while her legs began to shake.

"We need to sit you down," Nurse Walters said calmly as she slowly walked her towards a row of seats.

"I couldn't cope without Roy," Phyllis muttered as Nurse Walters helped her to sit down. "I won't have anyone judging me."

Nurse Walters could see that Phyllis was sweating and was taking short, sharp, breaths.

"We need to calm you down, Mrs Larner," Nurse Walters said as she stroked her shoulder. "How do you feel?"

Phyllis wiped the tears from her eyes and smudged her black eye make-up. She closed her eyes tightly and then looked upwards.

"Mrs Larner, can you hear me?"

"Sometimes I just feel like nothing is safe," Phyllis mumbled. "Whatever happens I mustn't lose control or all will be lost."

"Mrs Larner, you must tell me how you feel," Nurse Walters said firmly.

"I feel numb and dizzy and it's like I'm going to pass out," Phyllis muttered while her upper body swayed slightly from left to right.

"Right, now listen to me, Mrs Larner," Nurse Walters said abruptly. "You are having a panic attack, which is not uncommon in this situation. What I need you to do now is to take some deep breaths, can you do that for me?"

Phyllis nodded weakly and began to take deeper breaths.

"Good, that's it," Nurse Walters said warmly. "I want you to focus on your breathing."

Nurse Walters sat with Phyllis until the symptoms of her panic attack were brought under control. She looked up to see the older nurse returning with a doctor.

"How is my son, Roy?" Phyllis said as she bolted up from her seat.

The doctor smiled warmly.

"Its Mrs Larner, isn't it?"

Phyllis nodded.

"Where is Roy? I want to see my son."

"Roy is safe now and his condition is being managed," the doctor said calmly.

"Condition? What condition?" Phyllis asked.

"Please calm down Mrs Larner and take a seat," the doctor said, motioning Nurse Walters to help her sit down. "Roy's heart stopped momentarily."

"Oh no, no, no," Phyllis wailed as she clasped her hands together, closed her eyes and began praying.

"He is stable now," the doctor said reassuringly. "I believe your son has a common lung condition called asthma. It causes occasional breathing difficulties"

"Asthma," Phyllis whimpered.

"Asthma can affect people of all ages," the doctor said.

"But Roy is just a baby," Phyllis said as a single tear rolled down her cheek.

"Asthma can strike at any time," the doctor said. "There are times when the condition starts during childhood and other times as an adult."

"What can I do?" Phyllis pleaded. "Can you cure my son?"

"Once we have Roy's condition fully under control and you return to London, I would suggest that you visit your GP and tell him exactly what happened here," the doctor said.

Phyllis nodded.

"I will do that."

"Good," the doctor said with a kind smile. "Now, you will have to keep an eye on Roy and should you witness signs of wheezing, breathlessness or coughing, then you are to seek help immediately. Can you do that?"

"Yes, yes I will do that," Phyllis said. "What kind of things can bring it on?"

"The asthmatic condition is a swelling of the breathing tubes that carry air to the lungs. It can happen at any time, but allergies to things like animal fur or pollen can act as a trigger," the doctor said before standing upright to straighten his back.

"We don't have any pets," Phyllis said.

"That's good. Now, cold air or smoke from an open fire or cigarettes have also been known to act as a trigger."

Phyllis nodded.

"What is the cure for asthma?" Phyllis said. "Is it an operation and how soon can it be done?"

The doctor shook his head slowly.

"Despite some major progress, there is no cure for asthma today, Mrs Larner. It's generally considered to be a long term condition. We have known of incidents where asthma will simply go away during teenage years but then come back again during adulthood. The symptoms can be managed with treatment and most people then go on to lead normal, active, lives."

"No cure," Phyllis muttered as she lowered her head. "Most people, but not all people, go on to have healthy, normal and active lives."

"Like I said, Mrs Larner, asthma is considered to be a serious condition but it can be controlled with treatment," the doctor said.

Phyllis inhaled deeply and then stood up straight and wiped the tears from her face.

"I will do whatever it takes to keep my son safe," Phyllis said defiantly. "Now, I would like to see Roy."

***

The Larner family returned to the top floor of their four-storey flat in Muswell Hill, London, once Roy had been nursed back to health. Phyllis saw the GP on the day of their return. The council, once aware of baby Roy's health condition, made arrangements for the family to be moved closer to a hospital in Peckham.

Chapter 2

The Ledbury Estate in Peckham, South East London, was constructed with giant concrete sections between 1968 and 1970. It is a large social housing estate comprising of houses, maisonettes and four thirteen-storey H-Shaped tower blocks, each with fifty six flats, and located close to the Old Kent Road, Tower Bridge and The Elephant and Castle.

"Roy, can you please not kick the football in the house?" Phyllis shouted from the kitchen.

"Can I go out please Mum?" Roy, now aged five, called back while he passed the 'Johnny Hotshot' ball from his left foot to his right.

Mum's friend, Costas Paphitas, had first bought Roy a football when he was four years old. Lee had been away serving a prison sentence for fraud. The football had been nicknamed 'Johnny Hotshot' because it was light and would burst easily. On the first day Roy took his new ball out to play with his friends, Simon Callene, Gary Beck, Andrew Percival and John Gibbons, and they had found a small patch of grass to play on. Roy and Simon had taken their tops off to use as goal posts. The lads struggled to control the light ball. Roy took a shot at the goal and Gary dived and missed. It was a goal which had the lads yelling 'Goal!' while running in circles punching the air. However the 'Johnny Hotshot' football landed in a bed of stinging nettles and burst. News of the burst ball reached Costas and he returned to the flat with a second ball.

"Not just yet," Phyllis said as she walked into the living to find Roy heading the ball repeatedly in the middle of his forehead while keeping his eyes open.

"But Mum, Simon is probably already out," Roy pleaded.

"Costas will be here shortly and he wanted to see you," Phyllis said as she took one of her Irish jig albums out and placed it on the two-tone cream and pale blue Dansette Bermuda portable record player.

"Oh no," Roy thought. *"I can't stand this racket. What's wrong with Radio One and 'Tiger Feet' by Mud or 'Teenage Rampage' by Sweet?"*

Phyllis carefully wiped the twelve-inch vinyl record before placing it on the turntable.

"Mum, do we have to listen to this?" Roy whined.

"Yes and I like it," Phyllis said abruptly.

The vinyl record began to spin. There was a slight crackle as the needle landed on the groove and before the *'Morrison's Jig'* fiddle tune played.

"Even Donny Osmond is better than this," Roy thought as he headed his ball several more times.

Roy watched as his heavily pregnant mum closed her eyes and swayed back and forth to the music.

"She always looks so happy when she plays these Irish jig records," Roy thought as he watched a warm, happy, smile spread across his mum's face.

19

There was a knock on the front door. Phyllis immediately turned the volume down and motioned for Roy to stop heading his football.

"Sit down," Phyllis said before checking her reflection in the mirror and racing down the hallway.

Roy could hear his mother talking to Costas in the hallway.

"Hello Roy," Costas said, smiling broadly and stepping into the living room.

"Hello Costas," Roy replied.

"How are you today and how have you been?" Costas asked as he sat on the armchair.

Roy had, since his first encounter with asthma in Clacton-on-Sea, spent an average of three months of each year in hospital with severe asthma attacks.

"I'm okay," Roy said as he juggled the football between his left and right hand.

"Would you like tea or coffee, Costas?" Phyllis asked, standing the doorway.

"Coffee, please, Phyllis," Costas said with a shy smile.

"Black with two sugars," Phyllis said before heading towards the kitchen.

"I see that you're still enjoying your football," Costas said as he glanced down at Roy's football.

Roy nodded excitedly.

"I love playing football," Roy said as he threw the ball into the air and caught it.

"There is a lot more to football than just the game," Costas said.

Roy placed the ball by his feet.

"How do you mean?" Roy said, swivelling on his seat to face Costas.

"Football can teach a person a great deal about the skills he'll need in life," Costas said. "Take teamwork for example. If you were to score the winning goal, that would make every member of the team winners too. There is no self-game in playing great football because being selfish with the ball will almost certainly lead to defeat."

Roy nodded.

"Simon and I are a good team. We pass, tackle and share the ball," Roy said as he visualised playing football with his friend. "I score a goal and then Simon does."

"There you go, teamwork," Costas said as he pointed to the window. "Life is a team sport too, because out there success will depend on your ability to work with others."

Roy nodded.

"Does that make sense?"

Roy continued to nod.

"To win at football and this crazy thing we call life, you need talent, but you must also have a passion for what you do and that could be anything. For example, the most successful market trader will be enthusiastic about whatever he's selling; he'll know about the products and their uses and so customers grow to trust him and in return the trader gains loyalty," Costas said. "So it's talent and passion, Roy."

Roy smiled.

"Great football requires discipline and a rock solid work ethic," Costas said. "Do you understand what I mean?"

Roy shrugged his shoulders and smiled.

"It means that you always turn up for team practice, rain, hail or snow, and follow the team rules. If you can do that on the football pitch and in your everyday life, it can only lead to success."

"I want to be a footballer when I grow up," Roy said proudly.

"I'm sure you'll do just great at whatever you develop a talent and deep passion for," Costas said just as Phyllis entered the living room carrying a mug of coffee.

"So what are you two talking about?" Phyllis said as she placed the coffee on the table.

"Football," both Roy and Costas said at the same time.

Costas blew over the steaming mug and took a small sip.

"Thank you," Costas said before turning back to Roy. "I understand you'll be starting school soon."

Roy nodded.

"Do you know what school it'll be?"

"Roy will be starting at St Francis Primary School in September," Phyllis said as she sat down in the armchair opposite Costas.

"Good, that's a very good school," Costas said enthusiastically. "I think it's in Friary Road? You'll enjoy that, Roy."

"All my friends will be going there too," Roy said, reaching down for his football. "We're going to play football every morning outside the flats before school and then again when it's all finished."

"He loves his football," Phyllis said, shrugging her shoulders.

Roy leapt off the settee and raced over to the window.

"Did you know that we can see Millwall's floodlights from here?"

Costas smiled and nodded.

"Maybe one day I'll take you to an Arsenal game," Costas said before taking a second sip of his coffee. "Would you like that?"

"I'd just love to go to any game," Roy said as he peered out of the window towards Millwall's ground.

"Oh I nearly forgot," Costas said as he reached into his jacket and produced three 'Shoot!' football magazines.

Shoot! was a popular weekly football magazine featuring news and stories on all aspects of English and Scottish football.

"Wow, Shoot!" Roy said excitedly as he reached forward to take the magazines. "Thank you, Costas."

"My local newsagent brings them in," Costas said awkwardly. "If you like, I'll pick them up again."

"Yes please," Roy said, thumbing through the magazine.

Costas turned to Phyllis.

"How are Chris and Brian?"

Phyllis smiled.

"They're out playing with their friends."

"I bet you'd like to be out playing football," Costas said as he turned to Roy.

Roy's eyes lit up.

"Can I go out Mum… please?" Roy said before placing the 'Shoot!' magazines on the table and reaching down for his football.

Phyllis shook her head and smiled.

"Go on then, but stay with your friends Simon, Gary and Andrew," Phyllis said. "If you start to get short of breath then you come straight home. Is that clear?"

"Yes, Mum." Roy said as he juggled the ball between his left and right hand.

"Yes Mum, what?"

"Yes Mum, if I feel the asthma coming on then I'll come straight home," Roy said as he headed for the door.

Costas looked down at his watch.

"I'll walk you down," Costas said before reaching into his pocket and handing something to Phyllis. "Get the children and yourself something."

"Thank you," Phyllis said, promptly putting it in her pocket.

"Do you want to stay and play with us, Costas?" Roy said, hopping from foot to foot.

"I can't today, Roy," Costas said as they walked towards the front door. "We can do it another time though."

"Do you promise?"

"Absolutely," Costas said as he patted Roy's head and then turned back to Phyllis. "Take care of yourself and the new baby."

Phyllis smiled.

"So what else can football teach you about life?" Costas asked as they walked down the stairs.

"Teamwork and discipline," Roy said with a broad smile.

"Well done," Costas said as they opened the main doors leading out onto the estate. "Self-confidence is another important life skill football can teach you."

"I'm not confident at all," Roy thought as he peered around him. *"Not unless it's playing football with people I know."*

"Roy!"

Roy turned to see Simon, Gary and Andrew racing towards him.

"Do you fancy a game of footie?" Simon said before stopping to take a few deep breaths

Roy beamed.

"Yeah!" Roy said as he turned to face them.

"On your head," Simon called out before throwing the ball towards Roy.

Roy headed the ball back to Simon who in turn headed the ball over to Andrew.

"I'll be off then, Roy." Costas said before striding towards a blue Ford Granada GXL.

"Thanks for the magazines," Roy called out after him.

"Nice car," Gary said as the lads watched Costas open the door, climb in and start the engine.

"Proper nice," Simon said.

"What is he, like your uncle or something?" Gary said.

"Yeah, kind of," Roy said as he bent down to pick up the football.

"I'm not sure if Costas is my uncle or not," Roy thought as the lads walked back to their make shift goal made with a red and white plastic road cone and a broken kerb stone. *"I know that I like him and he's always there to help out the family when Dad is away."*

***

Roy and his friends played football until the sun started to go down. Having imagined that they had just won the World Cup against Germany, the lads sat down on the grass.

"My mum and dad had a right barney last night," Andrew said, lying down on the grass with his hands behind his head.

"Was he late from the pub or something?" Simon said. "Mum goes mad if Dad says he'll be home at a certain time and then forgets."

"My dad is rarely at home," Roy thought. *"Mum says he's working away but we all know that he's in prison."*

"Mum had just done the washing up and she's walked in on Dad glued to the television watching those Pan's People dancing on Top of the Pops," Andrew said. "They were all dressed in these short white dresses with big red hearts over their... well you know..."

"Boobs," Simon yelled out with a laugh.

All the lads began to laugh.

"My dad watches Pans People too and makes all sorts of gurgling noises while they dance about," Simon said. "He told me that he fancies the blonde girl, Babs, but not to tell Mum."

"Babs is my dad's favourite too," Gary said.

"Guess what?" Andrew said sitting bolt upright. "Mum said we might be getting a telephone."

"Really?"

"Yeah, but," Andrew said lowering his voice, "I won't be allowed to use it. Mum says it's strictly for her and Dad's use only."

"You will use it though, won't you?" Simon said with a cheeky grin. "Well, if you lot get a phone then I can call you."

"That would be so cool," Roy said as he visualised himself chatting to his friends about football while it poured with rain outside.

"Maybe I'll ask Mum if we can get a telephone too," Roy thought as he chuckled with his friends.

"The World Cup will be starting soon," Roy said.

"When?" Simon said as he leaned forward to rest his chin on his elbows.

"June 13th in West Germany," Roy said.

"My mum and dad don't care about football," Gary said with a sigh. "Can I watch the games at your house?"

"Yeah, me too," Simon said.

"Don't forget me," Andrew said with a chuckle.

"I'll have to ask," Roy said.

"Your mum is really cool," Simon said. "She's bound to say yes."

"All I can do is ask Mum nicely," Roy said.

"I hope that Chris and Brian want to see the World Cup too," Roy thought as he imagined his brothers and friends all watching England winning game after game at his home.

Chapter 3

Roy started at St Francis Primary School in the September with his friends. Every morning, unless the heavens opened, the lads would meet outside to play football for half an hour before going to school. Their new teacher was met by loud booing as she told them that the school leaving age had been increased to sixteen years of age the previous year. Once the playful class had settled down, she went on to explain that the school day started at 9.00am sharp and would end at 3.30pm. There would a break time in the morning, an hour for school dinners in the dining room, and a second break in the afternoon. The school had three term times and the autumn term would end on the 20th December when the school would be closed for two weeks. The spring term commenced on the 5th January and ended on Good Friday. The teacher advised the class that there would another two-week break for Easter, which would then lead into the summer term that ended on the 18th July.

Simon had put up his hand to ask when the summer term started. The class cheered when the teacher announced that the summer break would last for a full six weeks.

Roy liked his teacher and enjoyed the lessons almost as much as playing football during break times. However the asthma attacks continued to dog his education as well as his love of playing football. Roy spent an average of three months each year receiving hospital treatment and medication to manage the condition.

There was an addition to the Larner family, Paul.

29

During the unusually hot summer holidays of 1976, Roy and his friends played out on the Ledbury Estate. It had been almost too hot to play football as it was one of the driest and sunniest summers of the century. With the television news relaying stories of a severe drought in Britain and Ireland, the council had workers on the estate turning off outside taps.

Roy and his friends were walking through the estate when Simon stopped and looked up at the sky.

"Do you think that's Concorde," Simon said, pointing to a plane soaring across the blue skies.

"Could be," Roy said as he wiped the sweat from his brow.

"It's hot," Gary said.

"Bloody hot," Simon said with a chuckle.

The lads all laughed and continued to walk until they arrived at the garages.

"We could probably play football by the garages," Roy said, bouncing his football several times.

"Look, there's a tap," Simon said as he pointed towards the wall between the garages.

"It's probably been turned off," Gary said with a sigh.

"Well let's find out," Simon said before jogging off towards the tap. "Last one there wears girl's pants!"

All the lads roared away after Simon, not wanting to be the object of jokes for the next ten minutes. All the lads came to a stop around the same time. Simon reached out and turned the tap. There was a dribble of water.

"I think it's still on," Roy said.

"Turn it some more!" Andrew said, motioning Simon to be quicker.

Simon made the final turn and a thick gush of water poured from the brass tap.

"Yeah!" the lads all cried shouted.

Simon was the first to cup his hands under the tap and then cover his face in the ice cold water.

"That was brilliant," Simon said, rubbing the cold water around his face and into his hair.

"Can I have a go?" Gary said.

"Sure," Simon said as he cupped his hands to collect the water. He turned to Roy and winked before swivelling abruptly on his heels and throwing the water in Gary's face.

There was a second's silence.

"Water fight!" Roy yelled.

The lads scampered around the garages collecting anything that could hold water. Roy found a black plastic plant pot while Simon discovered a short length of pipe that smelt of petrol in a garage that had been left with the door up and partially open. Gary followed him into the garage and grabbed a sponge while Andrew emptied a saucepan with a broken handle full of nuts and bolts.

The lads all dashed back to the tap and began to fill and soak their weapons and then chase each other, calling out to one another and laughing out loud. Roy had been soaked and was laughing so hard that he began to find it difficult, with the intense heat, to catch his breath.

"Oh no, not another asthma attack, please, please not again," Roy thought as he stopped running and bent forward and put his hand on his knees.

"Are you alright mate?" Simon asked.

Roy raised his right hand indicating that he was okay before closing his eyes and taking slow, deep breaths.

"I'm alright," Roy thought as the breathing became easier. *"It's a false alarm."*

The lads played water fights for over an hour. They were all completely soaked but returned to the estate with huge smiles on their young faces.

A blue Granada stopped on the opposite side of the road. The driver wound down the window.

"Roy."

Roy and the lads turned to see Costas smiling and beckoning Roy over.

"I won't be a minute," Roy said before checking for traffic and crossing the road.

"Are you enjoying this glorious sunshine?" Costas said as he removed his sunglasses.

"Yeah, we've been having a water fight," Roy said with a broad smile.

"Good," Costas said. "How is Mum?"

"She's fine. She still goes to church every Sunday and looks after me and my brothers," Roy said, turning to see if his mates were still there.

"She's a good mum," Costas said with a smile.

Roy nodded.

"Here," Costas said as he handed Roy a five pound note.

"Wow, what's this for?" Roy said as he looked down at the five pound note.

"This is one of the best summers ever, go and have some fun!"

"Thank you, Costas," Roy said as he stepped back from the car and watched the electric window start to rise.

Costas slipped the automatic gear shifter into Drive and turned briefly to Roy. He raised his hand, checked his rear view mirror, and then slowly drove away.

"Was that your uncle?" Simon said as Roy re-joined his friends.

Roy nodded.

"I'm going to get a car like that when I grow up," Simon said. "Maybe I'll buy your uncle's car."

"I want a Jaguar like they have on the Sweeney," Andrew said.

The Sweeney was slang for Sweeney Todd – Flying Squad. The TV show featured two hard edged detectives from the Metropolitan Police's infamous Flying Squad. They would pursue Jaguar driving villains using methods that were underhand, frequently violent and illegal.

"I'd like an Aston Martin like James Bond, with machine guns hidden behind the blinkers and a bullet proof shield that pops up when you're being chased," Gary said.

"Do you know what I'd do if I were your passenger?" Roy said with a grin.

Gary shrugged his shoulders.

"I'd press the ejector seat and watch you fly off up into the air," Roy said, before bursting into raucous laughter.

The other lads all joined in the laughter.

"Yeah, but then you would crash and get all smashed to bits because no one was driving," Gary said, putting his hands on his hips.

"I never thought about that," Roy said while the lads continued to laugh.

Roy bounced his ball on the ground several times and then threw it over to Simon to head into the air.

"What about if we get a Red Bus Rover ticket tomorrow?" Roy said.

The Red Bus Rover Ticket could be purchased at London Underground stations and provided under fourteens with unlimited travel on London Transport buses for one day.

"My neighbour did that last year," Simon said. "He reckons it cost about fifty pence."

"I'm up for it," Andrew said. "My granddad gave me some money last week."

"I think it'd be fun," Gary said.

"It will be," Roy said. "We need to set off early so we can get a full day in."

***

Roy returned home to find that his mum had been out while his youngest brother, Paul, was sleeping and brought the family food from the chippie. Residents of the Ledbury Estate would often treat themselves to a choice of battered white fish, steak & kidney pies or battered sausages with chips and lashings of salt and vinegar on a Friday night.

Lee, his dad, was at home. The family ate together, although Lee was in a rush to get changed and go out to the pub. In the background, on low volume, Phyllis had the Irish fiddle tune *'Swallowtail Jig'* playing on the record player.

"I'll have them later," Lee said as he closed the chip wrapping around his unfinished meal.

"Will you be going out with Dad?" Roy asked after Lee had left to get changed in the bedroom.

Phyllis shook her head before sweeping two-year-old Paul into her arms and rocking him gently to *'The Kesh Mountain Jig'*.

Roy picked up a copy of 'Shoot!' magazine and sat on the settee. He pushed himself back into the seat for comfort. He opened the magazine and began to read.

Moments later Lee arrived back in the living room wearing a pair of brown flared trousers and a cream coloured long sleeved shirt with a huge butterfly collar.

"What is that smell?" Roy said as he lowered his magazine.

"That pleasant aroma, son, is Brut, and it's like Henry Cooper says, 'You splash it all over'," Lee said, parading in front of the mirror.

"It smells like an old sofa that's been left out in the rain," Roy thought as he scrunched up his nose.

"Your mum loves it on me, don't you Phyllis?" Lee said, brushing down his trousers.

"Course I do," Phyllis replied without looking up.

"Well I haven't had a decent pint in a while so don't wait up," Lee said before disappearing out of the living room and off down the hallway.

Once in bed Roy found himself thinking about Costas and how he would liken the skills you need to play good football to the same as you need in everyday life.

"Costas has always said that you should be disciplined and self-confident to be a team player," Roy thought as he lay back on his pillow. *"I have to have the right attitude and be physically fit and aware of what's happening around me and last but not least, have passion. When I grow up I'm definitely going to be a professional footballer."*

***

The following morning Roy met with his friends outside the tower block. They purchased their all day tickets from the local newsagents. With adrenaline racing through their bodies they clambered on board the Routemaster bus and travelled into central London. During the day the lads jumped off one bus and ran to another as the glorious summer heatwave continued. They passed Marble Arch, Hyde Park, Oxford Street, Piccadilly Circus, Trafalgar Square and Big Ben by Westminster Bridge. The lads jumped off the bus and spent time in Trafalgar square feeding the pigeons and chasing them once the bird feed had run out. The day passed quickly with the lads stopping to share a large bag of chips a couple of bus stops from the Tower of London.

On their way back to the Ledbury Estate the lads concluded that it had been the best day ever. Two days after Roy's adventures on the Red Bus Rover, he suffered a massive asthma attack and was rushed into Guys Hospital where he remained under close supervision for four weeks. Phyllis would arrive at the hospital after seeing Roy's brothers off to school. She would stay for ten minutes and then rush off to start her part time job at Barclays Bank. During the afternoons Roy would sit on the window sill and stare down at London Bridge looking for his mum. Without fail Phyllis would finish work and return to bring Roy stickers for his football books and to spend time chatting before rushing home to prepare dinner for the family.

Chapter 4

"Over here, over here," Roy called out as he stormed towards the make shift goal.

Simon tackled the defender and slid the ball across as Roy side-stepped his opponent. The goal keeper bounced from left to right trying to anticipate the shot. Roy feigned a left cross before smashing the ball into the goal.

"Goal!" Roy yelled out on top of his voice.

It was the 7th of June 1977, and there was a jubilant torrent of celebrations across London and the nation for the Queen's Silver Jubilee. While millions of people lined the streets across the capital, the Ledbury Estate was one of four thousand areas in London holding a massive street party. Organisers had put scores of highly decorated tables in a row and hung Union Jack bunting from the lampposts. Mums from all over wore Union Jack pinafores while young children played happily in their homemade fancy dress outfits and waved their hand-held Union Jack flags. Wolf whistles filled the air from dads and lads when two teenage girls, Julie and Karen, joined the party in their fashioned short dresses made from Union Jack flags with white knee-high socks and heels.

At 1.00pm a twenty-one-gun salute could be heard from the Tower of London. It was followed by another in Hyde Park, and then a second twenty-one-gun salute from the Tower of London. Both adults and children cheered as the sound of the final salute faded.

In addition to an egg and spoon race, the organisers had arranged a series of both sack and three-legged races for the children. Roy and his friends had opted to play the five-a-side football and romped home with a six goal lead in the finals.

Roy and the lads were hot, sweaty and hungry as they walked back towards the long line of highly decorated tables.

"Just a minute," Roy said before stopping and reaching down to his sock for his inhaler.

An inhaler is a device that holds medication for asthma that you take by inhaling it. The medication, once inhaled, goes straight down into the airways to provide relief. Roy had been using an inhaler since he was three years old.

"Are you alright?" Simon asked with concern as he had witnessed Roy's asthma attacks before.

"Yeah, yeah I'm fine," Roy said as he stood upright and grinned. "We won didn't we?"

All the lads laughed and continued to walk towards the street party.

One of the neighbours had brought down their radio. The DJ played *'You're Moving Out Today'* by Carole Bayer Sager.

"Look at that lot," Gary said as he gazed at the mountains of sausage rolls, crisps, finger food, assorted sandwiches and rolls.

"I've never seen so much grub!" Andrew said, reaching out for a cheese and tomato roll.

"Me either," Gary said, biting into a sausage roll.

One of the mums, dressed in a Union Jack pinafore, poured the lads a paper cup full of orange squash each. They thanked her.

"Why don't we take some of this grub and go down to the camp in the garages?" Simon said as *'Telephone Line'* by the Electric Light Orchestra played on the radio.

All the lad's eyes lit up. The previous year the lads had built a make shift camp in the garages where they would go to talk rather than go home when it rained. During the lead up to bonfire night, Roy and the lads joined scores of other boys of all ages from across the estate in finding things to burn on Bonfire Night. Old pallets and wood were stored in the garages ready for the build. Roy had been amongst the first to enter the derelict buildings while on the hunt for wood. The lads had ripped down the doors, cupboards and floorboards and dragged them back to the garages for safe keeping. It was then that the lads decided to hold back some of the wood destined for the monster bonfire and build a camp to hang out in. One enthusiastic lad, Nick Wood, from another part of the Ledbury estate, was trawling through burnt wood when he stepped on a rusty nail. Nick had yelled out in pain as the sharp nail ripped through the sole of his trainer and buried itself deep into his foot. Roy and Simon bolted through the garages and across the estate to the chippie where they explained what had happened and asked the owner to call an ambulance. The ambulance crew arrived in minutes and quickly whisked Nick off to the hospital.

"Sure, why not," Roy said as he began to pile sandwiches and homemade jam tarts onto his plate.

With a mountain of food the lads left the street party and piled into the camp.

"So why are you changing schools?" Simon said before ramming a full sausage roll into his mouth.

"I don't want to," Roy said as he looked at his sandwich and then put it back on his plate. "I just don't have a choice."

"Why?" Gary asked as he popped a cocktail sausage into his mouth.

"It's my asthma," Roy said with a heavy sigh. "They said because I've lost so much school time I need to go to a school where they have a full time nurse."

"Mate, I'm gutted," Simon said with his mouth still full of food. "Where are you going?"

"Brent Knoll School in Sydenham," Roy replied.

The Brent Knoll School catered for children with difficulties. Roy had been assured that the smaller classes and having a nurse on site, full time, would help to manage his asthmatic condition.

"Are we still going to play football every morning before school?" Simon said as he swallowed the last of his food.

All eyes were on Roy.

"I think so," Roy said, shrugging his shoulders.

"We'll just have to get up earlier then," Andrew said with a broad grin.

"What's that noise?" Simon said as he motioned the lads to be quiet.

"It sounds like a bunch of angry bees," Roy said before leaning forward to peer out between the planks of wood.

Walking through the garages were four teenage punk rockers carrying a hand held cassette player with *'God Save the Queen'* by the Sex Pistols playing at full, but muffled, volume.

Roy and his friends watched intently through the cracks and gaps in their camp as the three lads and the girl passed them by. The punk rocker carrying the cassette recorder wore black jeans with tears in the legs held together with large safety pins. His black T-Shirt had 'Anarchy' written across it in white paint. The punk's hair was a thick black pointed mop with electric blue dye on the tip of each point. He had his arm around a girl wearing skin tight red tartan trousers with black Dr Marten boots. Her black T-shirt had rips held together with scores of safety pins and 'No Fun' written on it in white paint.

"What the hell are they?" Gary whispered while watching the group traipse up the garages.

"Punk Rockers," Roy said.

"What you mean, like Johnny Rotten?" Simon said as he turned back to Roy.

Roy nodded.

"I saw them on that 'Today' program last year before Christmas and they were swearing their heads off," Roy said.

"What proper swearing?" Andrew said with an astonished look.

Roy nodded.

"What did they say?" Andrew asked softly, looking from left to right.

Roy took out his inhaler and inhaled the medication.

"He called Bill Grundy a dirty fucker," Roy whispered.

"Never," Andrew said. "They actually swore on television?"

Roy continued to nod.

"Did they say anything else?" Simon asked before pushing a second whole sausage roll into his mouth.

"They said shit and bastard," Roy whispered.

"I bet your mum went mad, what with her going to church and stuff," Simon said.

"She didn't hear it," Roy said with a chuckle. "She was in the kitchen, cooking."

"I think they look cool," Gary said.

"No way, they look a right state," Simon said

"Here, what do you call a punk hitchhiker?" Roy said with a grin

All the lads shrugged their shoulders.

"Stranded," Roy said with a raucous laugh.

Once Simon had stopped laughing, he took a deep breath and looked around at his friends who were still picking at their food.

"What do you call a boomerang that doesn't come back?" he asked, reaching for a cocktail sausage.

Roy was the first to shrug his shoulders.

"A stick," Simon said with a chuckle.

The lads feigned a laugh.

"Gary, do you want my jam tart?" Roy said as he lifted it from the plate.

Gary beamed.

"There you go," Roy said as he lobbed the jam tart across the camp, hitting Gary on the side of the face.

There were a few seconds silence before all four of the lads, shrieking with laughter, began throwing food at each other. Roy caught a jam tart square on the nose while Simon had several cocktail sausages bounce off his head. Andrew had an open lemon curd sandwich stuck to his cheek.

***

Roy's final days at St Francis School passed quickly along with the summer holidays as he played football daily with his friends. The first day at Brent Knoll School arrived and on the first day Roy befriended Dario, an Italian lad of the same age. They both shared a passion for football and were both quickly drafted into the five-a-side football team. Roy and Dario became best school friends.

Chapter 5

"One adult and one child to Wandsworth please," Phyllis said as she handed the bus driver a handful of change."

Once Phyllis had the two tickets, Roy followed his mum to the back of the bus where he sat down by the window.

Roy's father, Lee, had been found guilty of another fraud charge and had been sentenced to prison. He was currently being held at one of the UK's largest prisons, HMP Wandsworth. It is a category 'B' prison in South West London.

"I want to see my dad, but I don't like prisons," Roy thought as he stared out of the window at the swarms of shoppers and people going about their daily business.

"Are you okay, Roy?" Phyllis asked.

"Yes Mum," Roy replied, still staring out of the window.

"Prison must be full of extremely bad people like murderers," Roy thought. *"I don't want to visit a place like that and I don't want my dad to be in there either."*

Roy, aged ten, and his mum had boarded the number 37 bus from Peckham town centre.

"You make me really angry, Dad," Roy thought as he clenched his fists. *"Mum is always working either part time at Barclays Bank or looking after me and my brothers and you're not there to help!"*

The bus passed through Nunhead, stopping every so often to let travellers on and off the bus. Roy remembered the last time he had visited his dad in a prison. He found the buildings, uniformed prison officers and the succession of locked doors daunting, intimidating and frightening. Roy had visions of the lines of visitors waiting to be searched and processed by the strict procedures. His young heart pounded furiously as he passed by the huge, menacing looking, prison officer into the visiting room. He had seen his dad dressed in prison uniform sitting at a table. Roy heard the clunk of the door closing and being locked behind him. He had quickly scanned the room to see people of every age, race, colour and creed chatting with their loved ones.

"You should be at home and working a proper job to help Mum with the bills," Roy thought as the bus passed through Brixton.

Roy sighed heavily.

"Roy, are you sure you're okay?"

Roy nodded.

"You don't have to go in if you don't want to," Phyllis said.

"I'm alright Mum," Roy replied.

Roy had vivid memories flash back after his last visit. Both Phyllis and Roy were extremely tired when they left the prison. Phyllis seemed more stressed than usual and angry that again Lee had broken the law and was serving time in prison. Roy had felt sad that he had to leave his dad behind to be locked away with dangerous men. After standing in the vandalised, leaking, bus shelter for almost an hour in the pouring rain, they boarded the first of three busses that had arrived together, to travel the hour-long journey back to Peckham. The overall experience had left him feeling angry, anxious and desperately upset. When they got home, Roy had feigned the need to go to the toilet. Once inside the bathroom, with the door firmly locked, the tears had steamed down his face.

The bus passed over the bottom of Brixton Hill and continued to Clapham Common.

"At least I've got a proper football game to look forward to tonight," Roy thought as a sudden rush of excitement washed his negative thoughts away.

Costas was an avid Arsenal supporter. Roy was still completely mad about all things football but had not yet settled on a team to follow. He was thrilled when Costas arrived at the family home saying that he two spare tickets, one for Roy and one for a friend. Roy had offered the place to Andrew and he accepted immediately. The two boys jumped excitedly on the spot at the prospect of watching first division football.

The bus came to a halt in Wandsworth just as memories of a conversation he had heard a few weeks came back. Two women in the chippie queue had been talking about the potential return of the death penalty and about an eighteen year old called Francis Forsyth who had been executed at HMP Wandsworth in 1960.

"I hope they don't execute my dad," Roy thought as he crossed the busy road with his mother.

The authorities had contacted Phyllis, advising her that she had a visiting order and there was also one for Roy. While Lee had been on remand awaiting trial he had been allowed three – one hour visits per week. However, now that he had been convicted it had been reduced to just two one hour visits every two weeks.

The one hour visit passed quickly with Phyllis and Lee chatting about what was happening at home. Lee had asked Roy how he was and what he was up to at school, but after that the conversation remained between his parents. Roy gazed around the room at the sea of convicted prisoners happily conversing with family before images came up of the same men being herded into cells and having the door slammed shut and locked behind them.

While travelling back to Peckham, Roy thought about the game he would be going to later. Images of Pat Jennings leaping between goal posts to save the match came flooding in, along with defender Pat Rice and the forwards Alan Sunderland and Frank Stapleton driving the ball relentlessly through the defence and placing the ball firmly in the back of the net.

Back on the Ledbury Estate, Andrew had been waiting on the stairs by the front door. He had been so excited he just had to leave his home to be with his friend. Costas arrived right on time, as promised. Once he had spoken with Phyllis about the boys and how she was, the three football fans left the flat for Roy's first division one adventure.

"Somebody said your dad was in prison for having fake five-pound notes, is it true?" Andrew whispered as they walked down the stairs.

"I don't know," Roy replied.

"My dad said he wished he could have had some," Andrew said with a broad smile.

"It didn't do him a lot of good if he did have those fake fivers," Roy thought. *"What with being locked up every day and not being allowed to see your family."*

"Like I said, I don't know," Roy said bluntly.

"I didn't mean anything by it," Andrew muttered. "Can you imagine having stacks and stacks of fake five pound notes and just passing them off in shops and that?"

Roy nodded and chose not to continue the conversation.

Costas led the friends to his work van. He would normally visit in his Ford Granada but an urgent delivery had to be made and as a self-employed business owner, Costas loaded the van with garments from the warehouse and then drove them to his market trader customers in East London.

Once the boys were in the van, Costas started the engine.

"This is going to be a good game," Costas said with a broad smile.

Arsenal was playing Leeds United in the second round (2nd leg) of the Football League Cup at their home ground in Islington.

"What do you think the score will be?" Costas said as he changed gear and slowed to a stop at the traffic lights.

"I reckon it will be 2-0," Roy said with a wry grin.

"Well the second round first leg away game at Leeds last week was 1-1 so I'm going to be cautious and say 2-1 to Arsenal," Costas said as he gently eased the van away from the green lights.

"I think it will be a complete slaughter and Arsenal will win with a 4-0 score," Andrew said tapping the dashboard with the palm of his hand.

"That would be good, but I don't think so," Costas said shaking his head. "Don't get me wrong because I'd love to see the Arsenal boys smash four good, solid, goals in the back of the net, but I'm sticking firmly with 2-1."

"We'll see," Roy said as he sat back in his seat.

"Was everything okay today?" Costas said as he checked his rear view mirror.

"Fine, thank you," Roy said.

"Please don't ask about my dad being in prison with Andrew in the van." Roy thought.

"How is school?"

"It's great," Roy said, sitting up straight. "I have a good friend, Dario, and we play five–a-side football almost every day."

"Good and what about your lessons?"

"I like them too," Roy said. "The sports teacher said that we've been the best five-a-side team ever."

"I'm pleased for you Roy," Costas said. "Always be confident in who you are and you won't have to bend to peer pressure just to fit in and then people will come to you."

"Yeah, like Dario," Roy said.

"That's it, just like your friend Dario," Costas said while changing up into third gear. "It's a fact of life that you will not always get along with everyone so a smart person like you can learn to disagree with somebody without taking any personal offence. Do you understand?"

Roy nodded.

"You're a good lad, Roy," Costas said before covering the brake and turning his indicator on.

"I'm so excited," Roy thought as he looked ahead at the London traffic. *"We're actually going to a football stadium to see a game."*

Costas slowed down at a set of traffic lights. He was at the front of the queue.

Is there anything on the radio?" Andrew said.

Costas reached down and turned the radio on. He left it on low volume while *'I Only Want To Be With You'* by The Tourists played.

"Do you like this kind of music, Roy?" Costas asked while he watched the traffic lights change at the junction and traffic move forward.

"Yeah but I prefer Ska," Roy said.

"Ska?" Costas asked with a quizzical expression.

"Yeah, you know, two-tone music like Madness and The Specials," Roy said.

"Yeah, me too," Andrew said. "Two-tone is just the best."

"I don't think I've heard any of it," Costas said, shrugging his shoulders.

"It's unmistakable," Andrew said. "There's nothing else like it."

"Do you have any, what was it, Madness records?" Costas said as he slipped the gear lever into first gear.

"No," Roy answered.

"I'll pick you up a couple," Costas said as the lights changed from red to amber to green.

Costas shifted the gear lever into second gear when SMACK!

The whole van shuddered as a green Jaguar XJ6 accelerated after the traffic lights had turned to red and crashed into the side of the van. Andrew yelled out as he hit his head on the side window when the collision took place. Costas had been thrown forward and then slammed back in his seat. Roy felt the horrendous impact but had remained firmly in his seat.

Costas looked over at Roy.

"Are you alright, Roy?" Costas mumbled

"I think so, what happened?" Roy said

"I'm bleeding," Andrew said as he dabbed the cut under his eye and looked down at the blood on his fingers.

Costas pulled himself together and opened the van's door. He staggered around to the front of the van and looked at the green jaguar that was still buried in the side of his work van. The traffic edged past the accident.

"I'm sorry mate," the Jaguar driver called out of the driver's side window.

"You jumped the traffic lights," Costas said. "Look at the state of my bloody van!"

"I think the throttle cable must have stuck," the Jaguar driver said.

Roy watched as Costas appeared to get ready to launch into the driver then he just stopped, took a deep breath, and stepped away from the car.

Moments later a police car and an ambulance arrived. Andrew was taken to hospital with his cut eye. The police took details of the accident and one witness stayed behind to provide a statement. The van was bent like a banana and undrivable. The police arranged for it to be taken away. Costas and Roy went to the hospital where Andrew had received several stitches. They missed the game at Arsenal.

"I thought you were going to bash that Jaguar driver up," Roy said. "You looked really angry."

"I was very angry. That was a new van and that accident didn't need to happen," Costas said firmly.

"I'm pleased that you didn't beat up that Jaguar driver," Roy thought. *"I don't want you to go to prison too."*

"If I got angry with that driver and started swearing at him or making threats, he would have stopped feeling sorry about what he had done and focused on what I was saying. What's done is done. You and I are fine. Andrew has a couple of stitches and the van is just a metal work horse. It's fully insured so I'll just get another. It's

53

always a good idea to take a few moments to think about a situation before losing your temper," Costas said.

"I suppose the game will have ended," Roy said dropping his head.

"Don't worry I'll take you to another game, and soon," Costas said. "Both of you; that's if your parents let me, Andrew."

Costas turned to a passing orderly.

"Here mate do you know what the Arsenal score was?" Costas said.

"Yeah, 7-0 to Arsenal," the orderly said with a huge grin. "We absolutely battered them!"

Chapter 6

During the summer of 1980 Phyllis bought all her sons bikes on finance. Roy was thrilled with his MK2, Blaze Blue, Raleigh Grifter with the longer rear mudguard. It was the bike everybody in school and on the estate talked about and wanted.

Simon also had a bike and had met up with some other lads from the area. He had been told of an excellent track to race bikes around up on Jews Hill, an area nick named by the locals, where the old New Cross stadium stood. Roy, Simon and six other lads all rode off the Ledbury Estate and down the Old Kent Road and into Ilderton Road towards the industrial wasteland and Jews Hill.

"This is brilliant!" Roy thought as he surveyed the small hills and sharp twists and turns on the well-worn track.

Simon suggested that the lads rode around the track just the once to get used to its layout and then they should race against the clock. One of the lads was wearing a Timex watch with a second hand and so he'd been unanimously nominated to time every rider and then Simon would time his lap.

Roy was the second lad to stamp down his time on the make-shift race track. He reached down into his sock and took out his inhaler and breathed deeply. He wanted to be ready to put down the winning lap on his Blaze Blue Raleigh Grifter.

The lad with the watch stood by Roy's right hand side. He peered down at his watch and then over at Roy.

"On your marks... Get set... go!"

Roy raced off the line, pedalling with all the power his legs could muster. He loved the feel of his Raleigh Grifter despite it being chunky, heavy and a little cumbersome. Roy imagined it being a motorcycle as he turned sharply into the bends while twisting the handle grips to shift gear. With sweat pouring from his forehead Roy raced over the agreed finishing line with a very respectable time for his first race around the track.

While the rest of lads took their turns to lay down a race time he couldn't help but notice a stream of boys and young men congregating at the top of the hill.

"What's going on there?" Roy thought.

He looked back as another lad sped over the finishing line on his well-worn purple Raleigh Chopper with the Sturmey Archer 'T' gear-shifter. However, curiosity had got the better of him.

"Simon," Roy said.

"What?"

"I'm going to ride up there and see what's going on.

The crowd had grown to around fifty young men and boys.

Simon handed the watch to another of the lads.

"Hold on," Simon said. "I'll come with you."

Roy and Simon pedalled up towards the growing crowd. They stopped their bikes at the edge of the bustling crowd and looked down to see the Den.

"Millwall must be playing," Roy said as he clambered excitedly off his bike and put it on its stand.

"Yeah and we can see most of the ground for free!" Simon said.

Roy watched spellbound as Patrick Cuff strolled across the pitch to the goal. Melvyn Blythe, defender, was the next to take up his position, quickly followed by midfielders David Martin and John Seasman.

"This is brilliant!" Roy muttered as he watched Millwall's forwards take up their positions on the pitch.

"Here, Roy," Simon said pointing towards the football ground. "It's Anthony Kinsella!"

Roy smiled.

"That will be me one day," Roy thought as the referee blew his whistle and the home game began.

Roy was thoroughly enthralled throughout the game. A goal was scored by Millwall and all the 'free viewers' leapt into the air yelling out 'Yes!' from the tops of their voices. Roy punched the air several times as the adrenaline raced through his body.

"This is it," Roy thought as he looked around at the bright, euphoric faces around him. *"I'm nailing my allegiance to Millwall Football Club. They are now my team for life!"*

Chapter 7

Roy was in his bedroom thumbing through some old 'Shoot!' magazines.

"Roy, Roy," Phyllis called out.

"Yes Mum," Roy replied without looking up from the article he had just begun reading.

"Can you come in here please?"

Roy read to end of the sentence and then placed the magazine down on his bed.

"I'll read this later," Roy thought as he got off his bed and sauntered through to the front room.

Roy was a little taken aback when he saw his mum and Costas standing together.

"This looks serious, Roy thought as he sat down on the settee. *"What have I done wrong recently?"*

"Costas and I have been talking, and we think it's about time that we all had a chat about the real facts of life," Phyllis said.

"Mum I know all about the birds and bees," Roy said with a wry grin.

"I'm not talking about relationships and the importance of being respectful and properly prepared," Phyllis said with a hint of embarrassment.

"She's talking about rubber johnnies," Roy thought, desperately holding back a snigger.

"What your mum is trying to say, Roy, is that you're very close to becoming a teenager and it's important that you learn some life lessons," Costas said with a half-smile.

"Okay," Roy said as he pushed himself back into the settee.

"When some people see a group of teenagers strutting down the road laughing, joking and messing around with their friends as threatening, they would probably cross the road," Costas said.

Roy nodded.

"Young lads, in particular young lads from council estates like the Ledbury can often be viewed as troublemakers, yobs or hooligans," Costas said as he shrugged his shoulders.

Phyllis nodded her head in agreement.

"I've crossed the road myself on occasions," Phyllis said.

"A group of lads can walk into a shop and immediately members of staff will have their eyes on you because they think you've come to steal from them," Costas said as he rubbed his chin. "Does that make sense to you?"

Roy nodded.

"Where are we going with this?" Roy thought as he glanced up at the wall clock.

"I have even seen signs saying only two teenagers allowed in the shop at any one time," Phyllis said.

"I've seen that too," Roy thought.

"The message states that teenagers are not to be trusted," Costas said. "They can be seen as lazy, threatening and reckless.

"That's not fair is it?" Roy said. "I mean, sure there are a few people on the estate that do go nicking stuff from shops but that isn't everyone."

"True," Costas said. "The point is that not everyone has an open mind. Being a teenager can be difficult to say the least and being one from a London council estate has challenges that are not experienced by everyone."

"You mean boys from the big posh houses," Roy thought.

"When your mum and I were younger there were Mods and Rockers," Costas said. "The Mods wore smart clothes and rode around on scooters, while the Rockers wore heavy leather jackets and tore around the streets on noisy British motorcycles. On Bank holidays the Mods and Rockers would go down to Brighton, Margate or Southend and inevitably there would be trouble between the two factions. Now if you believed everything the newspapers wrote, then it was all out war, with both factions fighting each other and then the police. Well it simply wasn't true. Sure, there was the odd little fracas, but nothing like the newspapers would have you believe."

Roy looked at Costas questioningly.

"This all adds to the misconception that almost all teenagers are troublemakers," Costas said. "Now this is where the police come in."

"The police?" Roy said.

"Yes, son, the police," Phyllis said.

"You will have heard stories about the police around the estate," Costas said.

"Yes," Roy said while nodding his head.

"I've heard that you don't speak to them," Roy thought.

"I'm not going to tell you that all police officers are not to be trusted because that wouldn't be fair, but, and this is extremely important for you to understand, there will be those bad apples amongst them that will bend or even break the law to make arrests and build a career," Costas said. "Now when it comes on top the good law abiding police officers will, almost always, take the side of the bad apple and back him up so eventually you end up with a rotten barrel."

Roy looked shocked.

"I had a friend, a good friend who was arrested for the murder of a prostitute in Kings Cross," Costas said. "He was taken into custody after they battered down his front door, grappled him to the floor and handcuffed him in front of his wife and children. While at the police station several uniformed officers battered him senseless while trying to get him to confess to the murder. I am talking about a proper beating here, Roy, not just a minor scrap outside the pub. I mean a relentless kick after kick and punch after punch and all the while trying to get him to sign a confession."

"What happened?" Roy said as he watched his wide eyed mother place her hand over her mouth and sit down on the armchair.

"They threw him, battered and bruised, into a cold dark cell where he was left without food or water for seven days," Costas said as he lowered his head.

"Seven days!" Roy said.

"He had to drink the water at the bottom of the toilet bowl," Costas said.

"Oh my," Phyllis said as she placed her hand over her mouth.

"They finally let him out when a police officer came forward and admitted to the murder, claiming it was some kind of game they played with a rope but I won't get into all that," Costas said.

"That's terrible," Phyllis said.

Costas nodded.

"My friend had to hobble with multiple broken and fractured bones the half mile to the closest hospital."

"Did he report them?" Roy asked.

Costas shook his head.

"There would have been no point and he knew that," Costas said. "He was a working class lad that fitted the profile and they wanted to nail that crime on him regardless of him being innocent with a cast iron alibi."

Roy sat in silence and thought about the innocent man locked away in a cell for over a week.

"You will have friends, Roy, who will look up to what they perceive as success on the estate. You may even be doing that yourself," Costas said.

Roy immediately thought about the brothers Dougie and Nicky Worsfold. They both drove around in flash cars, wore good clothes and always had women chasing after them. Roy knew, from talking with friends, that they were both villains.

"Their path is laid out before them and they will, almost certainly, end up either dead or locked away for a long time and your mum and I do not want that to happen to you," Costas said, fixing his eyes on Roy.

"I don't do anything bad, honest," Roy said.

"We both know that you're a good lad who enjoys nothing more than his football but temptation will present itself and you need to be conscious of the decisions and choices you make," Costas said.

"I will," Roy answered while still thinking about the badly beaten man locked away in a cold cell without food or water.

"We don't want to see you in trouble with the law, or worse still, locked away in prison," Phyllis said.

"That's right, so obey the law, Roy. Only the truly rich and powerful ever get to blatantly break the law and walk away."

Roy nodded.

"There will be times when you will be very tempted to take the law into your own hands," Costas said. "It may be that a friend gets off with your girlfriend or a couple of drunken lads start acting up. Think twice before simply laying into them. People can be incredibly fragile and a punch, kick or whatever could have you looking at a life sentence in prison. I had another friend, nice guy who did a lot of body building. He would do door work, you know a bouncer."

Roy nodded.

"Well a couple of lads started acting up after one drink too many and my friend grabbed one of them by the scruff of the neck and threw him out of the club. Well the lad has landed awkwardly and bashed his head on the concrete kerb. The ambulance arrives and the lad is dead. My friend ended up doing ten years inside for that. The lesson here is to avoid, if possible, taking the law into your own hands."

"Ten years!" Roy thought as he imagined the bouncer being carted off in a police car.

"This next one will be extremely tough on you and most of the lads from council estates," Costas said. "Avoid bad friends. By all means say hello and even exchange a few words but don't hang out with these people. You have to believe me when I say that most of the people banged up in the nick are there because of the company they kept. Do not allow yourself to be lured into a life of regret."

"Okay," Roy said as images of his friends from around the estate entered his mind.

"If it feels wrong, Roy, then just don't do it," Costas said. "Always trust your instincts and say what you mean, and by that, I mean do not be afraid to say no. Finally, avoid drama like the plague. It will only ever end up one way."

Roy nodded as the words sank in.

"It's important to become a person that adds value to society despite all its flaws. You visited your dad in prison, didn't you?" Costas said.

"Yes, I did," Roy said as he remembered the bus journey to Wandsworth.

"Well, we don't want to make that journey to see you locked away, okay?" Costas said. "It would break both our hearts."

Roy could feel a lump developing in the back of his throat.

"I won't be going to prison, I promise," Roy said as a single tear ran down his cheek.

"Always remember that there is no such thing as easy money without risk. Robbery can get you quick cash and the perception of happiness, but it can also lead to years of your life being banged up behind locked doors," Costas said. "We love and care for you Roy, and want you to take on-board what we've spoken about today, and if you need to chat at any time then we are both ready to listen and help in any way we can."

"Thank you," Roy said as the tension around the room subsided. "I do understand what you're saying and I promise you that I'm not a troublemaker."

"We know that," Phyllis said. "So, what are you up to today?"

"I'm going outside to play football while the weather is still good," Roy said as he got up from the settee.

"I thought you might like to come up to Hertfordshire to help me and your mum in the warehouse next weekend," Costas said.

"Okay," Roy said with a broad smile.

"We could do some fishing too," Costas said as he watched Roy leave the front room.

"See you later," Roy called back before closing the front door behind him.

Roy scampered down the stairway before pushing the doors open to the outside. He was surprised to not find his usual friends playing football. However, his friend, Karl, who lived in the same bock of flats, was sitting on the roadside kerb throwing small stones at a discarded fizzy drink tin.

Roy was just about to call out to his friend when he looked up to see Concorde fly over.

"Wow," Roy thought as the magnificent aircraft flew over. *"I'll be a passenger on that one day."*

"Karl, how are you?" Roy said as he bounded over.

"Hello mate. Yeah I'm good," Karl said before throwing a final stone which sent the can flying across the road.

"What are you doing?" Roy said, sitting down on the kerb.

"I was just thinking about all those people who live out in the country," Karl said before shrugging his shoulders. "I mean, what on earth do they do out there?"

"They're probably kept busy looking after the farm animals and growing stuff," Roy said.

"Can you imagine waking up every day to just pick fruit from trees or feed the cows?"

Roy thought about it for a moment.

"No, I can't imagine not living in London," Roy said with a grin.

"Yeah, me too," Karl said, standing up and brushing himself down. "You can still get bored though mate."

"I don't know what you mean," Roy thought. *"As long as you have a ball and a few mates to play against what more do you need?"*

"I suppose so," Roy said as he stood up.

"I suppose you only get out what you put in," Roy said. "Costas told me that."

"Costas is a proper good bloke," Karl said. "He always gives my mum proper mate's rates for stuff when she sees him."

"Yeah, he is," Roy thought as the two lads turned away and began to walk across the estate.

The lads stood on the roadside and looked to their left when they heard the squealing of car tyres. A bright red Ford Capri came roaring into view. The lads could hear the high engine revs as the driver raced through the gears. Suddenly the driver hit the brakes and all the wheels locked up with grey tyre smoke belching out of all four wheel arches. The driver's side window was wound down and Patrick Bradley stuck his head out with a broad, mischievous, smile on his face.

Patrick and his family had moved over from Belfast several years back and from day one Patrick had been a handful. He would mess around in the classroom at school and become, according to the teacher, a class clown. Patrick was funny and could easily get the other kids in the class to follow him into doing something fun but naughty and against the school rules.

Karl, Roy, what are up to?" Patrick said in his broad Irish accent.

"Nothing," Karl said.

"What do you think of the motor?" Patrick said as he patted the driver's side door.

"Nice, very nice," Karl said as he stepped towards the car.

"It's a three litre Ghia, top of the range and boy, she doesn't half shift when you put your foot down," Patrick said as he revved the engine.

"Whose is it?" Roy asked.

Patrick shrugged his shoulders.

"It was parked up outside a telephone box and the keys were still in it," Patrick said with a broad grin. "It was like she was talking to me. Please Patrick, please take me away and run me ragged. What can I say? I had to oblige."

"She's a beauty," Karl said as he ran his hand over the gleaming red paintwork.

"Here, watch this," Karl said as he slammed the gear shifter into first gear and then covered the brake pedal lightly by arching his foot between the accelerator and the brake. He revved a couple of times and then dropped the clutch. The rear wheels spun while the engine roared. Thick tyre smoke belched out of the rear arches.

"You'll like this," Patrick yelled out as he let the car slowly slide sideways and edge up the road with tyre smoke pouring from the rear arches.

"Love it!" Karl said as he punched the air. "Now that is a proper burnout."

"That's what they make three litre Capri's for," Patrick said. "Do you want to get in and go for a smoke about? You never know, we meet find someone to race."

Roy could see Karl's eyes light up.

"Yeah, why not," Karl said as he raced around the car to the passenger side. "Are you coming Roy?"

Roy thought about it for a few seconds and then shook his head.

"Nah, I'm off to play football," Roy said.

"Come on Roy, it'll be a laugh," Patrick said.

"Nah, I'll catch you later," Roy said as Karl slammed the door shut.

Patrick revved the engine several times before dropping the clutch and screeching off sideways. Seconds later Roy heard the sound of police sirens entering the estate. He crossed the road and stood back as the police car sped by with its lights flashing.

Roy walked over to the other side of the estate with his hands in his pockets. It was then that he saw three lads playing football outside a block of flats.

"I wonder if they'll let me play," Roy thought as he approached the lads.

Roy had seen all three lads around by the fish and chip shop but he didn't know them to talk to. He sat down and watched the lads play and when the ball came his way he passed it back.

Finally one of the lads spoke to him.

"Do you fancy a game?"

Roy's eyes lit up.

"Yeah, great," Roy said as he got back on his feet and brushed the freshly cut grass off his trousers.

"I'm Tony, Tony Eagle and this is my brother Danny.

"Alright," Roy said with a friendly smile. "I'm Roy, Roy Larner."

"I've heard about you," Tony said. "You're supposed to be a good footballer."

Roy shrugged.

"Yeah and I'm Jack," the third lad said.

"Hello mate," Roy said.

Roy and the three lads played game after game and then finally sat down exhausted after Roy and Tony had won all but one of the games.

"Don't you get down to Millwall?" Tony said.

"Yeah, we watch the game up on Jews Hill," Roy said.

"Do you ever go and see the reserves during the week?" Tony said.

Roy shook his head.

"You should come, mate and they don't charge either. I just go into school and do my bit during the morning, have lunch and then shoot off down to see the lads play in the afternoon."

"I will," Roy said excitedly.

"It'll be fun, always is," Tony said. "My brother doesn't care too much for the game but it fills his day."

"Yeah, yeah, well we can't all be footballers when we grow up," Danny said.

"Is that what you want to be, you know, when you've grown up?" Roy asked.

Tony nodded his head.

"I'd love to play," Tony said. "What about you?"

"I can't think of anything I'd rather do than get paid to do what I love most in the world," Roy said.

"I'm in no rush to grow up," Jack said as he leant back on the grass and put both hands behind his head. "My sister's boyfriend told me that when you're old, you know thirty odd and all that, your ball bag hangs down to your knees and your knob shrinks permanently."

"No way," Danny said.

"Yep and then it just stops working altogether," Jack said as he placed a single blade of grass into his mouth. "True."

"Take no notice of him," Tony said with a chuckle.

"Here, do you remember that time Patrick Bradley nicked a bottle of whiskey from his house?" Jack said.

"Don't remind me," Danny said as he feigned being sick. "I never knew that you could bring up blue sick.

"It was horrible," Tony said. "I had one swig and that was it, but old Jack and Patrick just wolfed down the whole bottle."

"I've never drunk whiskey," Roy said.

"I've never had any alcohol," Roy thought.

"Trust me mate you haven't missed anything," Tony said before looking over at a young pretty girl with long dark curly hair coming out of the flats.

"Here Danny, Amanda Black is over there," Tony said.

"Where? Where?" Danny said as he sat bolt upright and looked around him. "Wow, she is beautiful."

"Yeah I suppose," Tony said.

"Well I heard that she was snogging Patrick Bradley in the garages," Jack said abruptly.

"I would love to play mummies and daddies with her," Danny sighed.

"I kissed her once," Jack said.

"No way!" Danny said.

"Yeah right, no way," Tony said firmly.

"It wasn't a full-on French kiss, but a kiss is a kiss," Jack said as he chewed on the blade of grass.

"I find that very hard to believe," Tony said.

"Alright, where and when?" Danny said, slapping his open hand on the ground.

"We were playing kiss chase at junior school and I caught her. So, a kiss is a kiss," Jack said with a broad smug expression.

"I hardly think that counts," Danny said.

"Well it's more than you matey," Jack said with a chuckle.

Danny reached out and grabbed a handful of freshly cut grass, got up and threw it at Jack. The four lads all burst out laughing.

Roy found himself thinking about the earlier conversation with Costas.

"There doesn't seem to be much respect or trust for the police on the estate. Why do you think that is?" Roy said as he turned to Tony.

Tony thought for a moment.

"They tend to act as though they have special rights and privileges and that can get right up people noses," Tony replied.

"Yeah, especially in a country where we're all supposed to equal," Jack said before taking the chewed up blade of grass from his mouth.

Roy was to become life life-long friends with his fellow Millwall supporter Tony and his brother Danny Eagle.

Patrick Bradley and Karl were arrested for multiple car related offences following a high speed chase across South East London. Patrick was sent to Borstal and Karl was placed on probation.

Chapter 8

February 16th 1980

Roy fumbled through his seven inch singles collection and settled on *'Night Boat to Cairo'* by Madness. He watched as the arm sprung up and settled the needle at the beginning of the track. There was a slight rumbling through the speakers as Roy had played the track over and over since Costas had bought him several Ska records.

Dressed in just his underwear, Roy waited patiently for the saxophone instrumental intro. Suggs, the lead singer of Madness, belted out the opening lyrics:

'Its just gone noon, half past monsoon

On the banks of the river Nile'

Instantly Roy closed his eyes and began to feel the beat before swinging his arms back and forth with clenched fists and doing the running man by bending his knees and running on the spot to the music.

Skanking is the style of dancing that is most popular with the two-tone rude boys.

"This is going to be brilliant!" Roy thought as he pictured Melissa, Dario's sister, holding up three tickets to see Madness perform a Saturday morning gig for the under 16s at the Hammersmith Odeon. Tickets were just one pound each

Roy and Dario had become great friends at school. His sister, Melissa, was a couple of years older and was an avid reader of The New Musical Express (NME) and Melody. She followed the music industry and had a love for the complex style of music with a plethora of cultural influences known as Ska. As soon as Madness announced their intention to put on a show for the under 16s, Melissa immediately bought three tickets.

Roy had first met Melissa while visiting Dario at home. His jaw fell open when he first laid eyes on her long locks of vulcanite-black hair that surged and flowed over her shoulders and shrouded her smooth, tanned skin. When she looked up from her magazine, Roy's heart skipped a beat when he saw her vivacious walnut brown eyes and Hollywood smile.

"Dario, your sister is absolutely stunning," Roy had thought.

The record finished, but the adrenaline and excitement continued to flow through Roy's body as he placed the needle back on the record.

Roy reached into his wardrobe for his two-tone tonic trousers. They had a shiny two-tone appearance and had first become popular with Mods and Skinheads.

"These are the nuts!" Roy said as he placed his right leg into the trousers. *"Thank you Costas."*

Roy pulled them up and checked out his reflection in the mirror as Suggs belted out:

'Only just one more to this desolate shore

Last boat along the Nile.'

He had asked his mum to iron his white Ben Sherman shirt with the button-down collar and inch wide pleat down the back with a tab.

"You've got to love a Ben Sherman," Roy thought as he pushed his arm through the long sleeve.

Roy did up the button and tucked the bottom of the shirt into his trousers before slipping his feet into a pair of black leather loafers with tassels.

"I feel like a million dollars," Roy thought as he turned sideways in front of the full-length mirror. *"Look it too!"*

Roy was just about to put the record back on for a third time when Phyllis, his mum, called out from the kitchen.

"Roy, can you not keep playing the same record over and over!"

"You mean like you do with that awful Irish jig stuff?" Roy thought as he placed the arm and needle back on its resting place.

The turntable stopped spinning and Roy put his treasured record back into its cover.

"Now for the icing on the cake," Roy thought as he reached over for his Crombie overcoat.

Roy had seen the coveted tailored overcoat in a charity shop in New Cross for just three pounds. He convinced the shop keeper to put it to one side for him for two days which gave him time to first speak with his mother and then with Costas who immediately gave him the money.

"You look the dogs dangly bits," Roy thought as he did a little skanking to the sounds of Madness in his head.

Roy looked over at the clock. With the concert due to start at 11.00am he had to get moving.

Roy took a long shot from his inhaler before slipping it into his inside pocket.

"See you later Mum," Roy called out as he opened the front door.

"Have a good time," Phyllis called back.

"I'm going to have the time of my life," Roy thought as he pictured himself standing with his best mate Dario and his beautiful sister, Melissa.

Unlike his friend Simon, Roy was incredibly shy around girls. When he shared this confidentially with Simon, he shrugged it off with 'just take a deep breath mate and push through it'. Roy had seen how Simon could just waltz over to a bunch of pretty girls and engage them in chat and within seconds he had them laughing and hanging on his every word. Despite Simon's fleeting advice, Roy would become physically anxious, scared and inhibited around most girls, especially those he liked.

By complete contrast, Roy found himself to be incredibly comfortable around Melissa. His mind would never go blank and he always knew what to say. After a short while he no longer saw her as this stunningly attractive girl, that humoured his weak jokes, but as an incredibly lovely person. They would talk about bands and music, and where the industry was going with the sudden influx of the New Romantic Movement. Roy, reluctantly, agreed to liking some of the Adam & The Ants music, although his first love remained Ska. Melissa would tell him how important it was to embrace the anarchic anti-punk change and live for the moment because it would never be repeated. Roy could listen to Melissa for hours but was unable to ever get up the courage to share how he felt about her.

Roy bounded down the stairs and then out onto the Ledbury Estate. Dario, in his stay press jeans, Ben Sherman merlot gingham shirt, black Harrington jacket and Dr Marten boots, waved.

"Roy!" Dario called out.

Melissa looked stunning in her short dress featuring large one inch square black and white diamond shapes all over, and black kitten heels.

"Damn!" Roy thought as she produced her heart melting Hollywood smile.

"Do we all look good or what?" Roy said, beaming.

"Not too shabby," Melissa said with a chuckle.

The bus to the Elephant & Castle arrived on time and within a matter of minutes the three Ska fans were travelling on the Bakerloo line where they changed to the District line at Embankment. They passed through Westminster, St James Park and Victoria.

"Did you see Madness on Tiswas?" Melissa said with a grin.

"Yeah, didn't they perform *'My Girl'*?" Roy said.

"They certainly did," Melissa said. "Do you watch Tiswas a lot then?"

"Yeah, well, sometimes," Roy said, feeling unsure about what he should be agreeing to.

"I love it!" Melissa said.

"Yeah, me too," Roy said with a wry smile.

"Not as much as our dad though," Dario said shaking his head.

"Really?" Roy said with a look of confusion.

"Yeah, he thinks we haven't noticed how he drools over Sally James," Dario said with a chuckle.

Sally James was an iconic presenter who had presented the popular seventies show, Saturday Scene, before moving on and bringing an unprecedented sex appeal to Tiswas (This is Saturday Watch and Smile) and joining Chris Tarrant and Trevor East as a presenter.

The underground train passed rapidly through Sloane Square, South Kensington, Gloucester Road, Earls Court, West Kensington, and Barons Court before reaching Hammersmith. The journey, with the change at Embankment, took just over half an hour.

Hammersmith station was awash with scores of teenagers milling about dressed in their two tone gear.

"We're in good time," Melissa said as she looked down at her watch.

"Other than going to Millwall, this has got to be one of the greatest feelings in the world," Roy thought as they crossed the busy road to join hoards of teenage rude boys and rude girls waiting to enter the Hammersmith Odeon.

The thought of seeing Madness performing some of his favourite songs of all time live on stage caused a sudden rush of adrenaline to race through his body.

Roy, Melissa and Dario lined up alongside the other excited Madness fans while they talked about the band, their music and the concert to come. With his heart racing, all Roy could think about was what was about to happen next.

Melissa handed over the tickets and they followed the crowds down towards the concert hall. They found their seats while all around them groups of dressed up two tone boys and girls chatted and laughed out loud. The lights lowered and everybody, including Roy, stood up and began to cheer at the top of their voices. Girls to his left and right shrieked while others burst into floods of tears as the lights lit up again and lead singer, Suggs, and the band bounded out on stage.

'Hey you, don't watch that

Watch this

This is the heavy, heavy monster sound

One Step Beyond'

The audience continued to cheer, shriek and scream as the band sang and danced around on the stage.

Roy was feeling overwhelmed at being entertained by his favourite band, listening to his preferred tracks live while being surrounded by fellow Madness fans and having the stunningly beautiful Melissa skanking by his side.

Roy smiled, danced and sang along to each and every song as if there were no one else in the concert hall. For the duration of the concert he was no longer Roy Larner from Ledbury Estate in Peckham but a Rude Boy enjoying the experience with like-minded people. For the first time he truly understood what Melissa had meant when she told him to 'live for the moment'.

The band moved swiftly from One Step Beyond to My Girl, Night Boat to Cairo, The Prince to Land of Hope and Glory. Just as Madness belted out their final song, the lights very quickly came on and the band left the stage to hoards of cheers and chants for the band to come back on and deliver more. It didn't happen so the concert was over and Roy, Dario and Melissa joined the rest of the fans who had been hit with post-concert depression.

"This will go down as one of the greatest moments in my life," Roy thought as they stepped aboard the tube train that took them back to Embankment.

Chapter 9

A week had passed and Roy still found himself thinking about the Madness gig at the Hammersmith Odeon. He had been enjoying school, especially the football. The sports teacher, Mr Bundy, had seen Roy's talent with a football and had used his network of contacts to enter the school into a London five-a-side tournament. The school had soared through the competition with Roy being the major goal scorer. On reaching the finals, the school team walked away with a 5-1 victory with Roy scoring four of the goals. There was a rumour that a major scout had attended the final game.

"Roy," Phyllis called out.

Roy was in his bedroom reading the latest edition of 'Shoot!'

"Yes, Mum?" Roy called back without looking up from his magazine.

"Costas is here," Phyllis replied.

"Costas, excellent!" Roy thought as he placed the magazine on the bed, took a short shot from his inhaler, and ventured into the living room.

"Hello Roy, how are you?"

"Yeah, I'm good," Roy said as he sat on the settee opposite Costas.

"I heard that you played well in that London Five-a-Side competition," Costas said.

"I did, I did, and I scored the winning goals," Roy said proudly, puffing out his chest.

"Well it seems that I'm not the only one who has been hearing good things about you," Costas said, raising his eyebrows.

Roy looked confused.

"I've been talking with some people I know at Arsenal and your name came up," Costas said with a broad grin.

"Really," Roy said as he sat bolt upright.

Costas nodded his head.

"You, Roy, have earned yourself a trial at Arsenal Football Club," Costas said calmly.

"You're joking," Roy said, his mouth hanging open.

Costas shook his head.

"I wouldn't joke about something as serious as this," Costas said.

"You did this for me, didn't you?" Roy thought as the news slowly sank in. *"I can't believe it. I've got my shot at playing professional football."*

"Well done Roy," Costas said as he patted him warmly on the shoulder. "Your love of the game, hard work, dedication and practice has paid off."

Roy was so excited he could have exploded on the spot.

"You're bound to feel a little nervous, but that's to be expected," Costas said as he stepped back and put his hands in his trouser pockets. "This opportunity could lead to a lifetime career."

Roy looked down at his hands, they were shaking.

"What will I have to do?" Roy said finally.

"Do what you do best," Costas said. "Play your heart out. But you will need to prepare."

Roy nodded enthusiastically.

"The trial starts next Monday at the Arsenal training ground at London Colney in Hertfordshire.

"Okay," Roy said as he fumbled with his fingers.

"Between now and then you will have to practice your passing, shooting, dribbling and ball manipulation, can you do that?" Costas said.

Roy nodded.

"I can do all that in my sleep," Roy thought.

"I want you to think about the games you've watched at Millwall and on the television and how the players communicate with the rest of the team and their style of play," Costas said. "I'm sure you've seen a good team lose badly and a rank outsider come through and win the day."

"I've seen plenty of that," Ricky said confidently.

"The thing is, Roy, football is so much more than just a player's technical ability," Costas said as he shook his head. "To stand the best chance in this trial you'll have to imagine yourself controlling the ball, creating opportunities and scoring the goal, while staying calm, relaxed and in complete control. You must enter this trial believing it to be a positive experience and that will help to calm any pre-trial nerves."

"I can do that," Roy said.

"Finally, you will need to be as physically fit as you can be, to be in the best possible shape," Costas said.

Roy's heart sank.

"What about my asthma?" Roy thought as he imagined himself on the playing field having to stop and use his inhaler.

"Practice your short sprints to improve your speed, acceleration and overall endurance.

Roy nodded.

"I know what you're thinking, Roy," Costas said softly. "I believe that you and one of the greatest and most respected naval commanders of all time, Lord Nelson, have some things in common."

Roy sat upright and listened intently.

"He was extremely brave and daring and despite losing his sight in one eye and suffering a multitude of injuries, he persevered, just as you will with your asthma, and went on to win all his battles and wars until he died."

Roy was stunned by Costas' analogy.

"I truly believe, with all my heart, that you have what it takes to do anything you put your mind to," Costas said, stroking his chin and smiling.

"Thank you," Roy said. "I promise to do my best."

"That, Roy, is all anyone can ever do," Costas said. "I'll take you to the training ground in London Colney nice and early on your first day, okay?"

***

Roy had listened to and implemented all of Costas' advice. He had practiced his short sprint back and forth in front of the flats and marked out spots on the wall with chalk and then dribbled the ball until he imagined a fellow team member being well placed and then passed. He was relentless until the football hit the chalk cross each and every time. His mind set was positive. Roy was ready for destiny to lead him through the trial and on to becoming a professional footballer.

Roy had been up early and was ready for when Costas arrived to take him out to London Colney on the first day of his trial for Arsenal.

"Nice car Costas," Roy said as he opened the door to the seven series BMW.

"I fancied a change," Costas said as he turned the ignition key and started the engine. "If you work hard and smart, Roy, choices will come your way."

Roy told Costas how he had been practising at every opportunity and was as ready as he could ever be.

"Do you feel confident?"

Roy nodded and smiled.

"*I just hope I don't have to use my inhaler,*" Roy thought as he turned to look out of the side window.

"Everything will turn out the way it's meant to," Costas said.

"*In that case I'll be signed on the spot and will be amongst the youngest ever professional footballers,*" Roy thought as a huge smile spread across his face.

"I'm excited, Costas, but despite everything you've said, I still feel a little nervous," Roy said as Costas slowed down for the traffic lights.

Costas turned to Roy.

"The best way to get through this is not to let the opportunity get the better of you," Costas said with sincerity. "It's essential that you remember that you were invited for this trial because a professional scout saw qualities in you that could add value to the team and the club. In short, Roy, you got the trial because you earned it."

Roy smiled.

"Did you work on your foot speed, straight line speed and speed endurance?" Costas said as he pulled away from the traffic lights.

"Every single day," Roy said.

"Well done," Costas said as they left London and entered Hertfordshire.

"Will there be a lot of us at the trial?" Roy asked.

"I'm sure there will be a lot of talented boys there," Costas said. "Remember though, this isn't a time to be making new friends. By all means be professional and polite, but your number one goal is to impress the recruiters. Once you've passed the trial you can make all the new friends you want."

"Okay." Roy said with a slight nod of his head.

"My stomach is churning like a spin dryer on maximum speed," Roy thought.

"Professional football, as you know, is highly competitive, so you must expect there to be a certain amount of pressure on you throughout this trial," Costas said. "Just go in there and express your love of the game with the skills that got you spotted in the first place, okay?"

"I will," Roy said as Costas slowed the car down and parked outside the training ground.

Roy's football trial ran from Monday to Friday. He hid his inhaler down his sock while playing. Costas had been right. There were a lot of extremely fast and talented players competing for the same opportunity that he was. Meeting the skilful goal keeper, Pat Jennings, Arsenal's top goal scorer, Frank Stapleton, and the legendary Bob Wilson had left him, momentarily, speechless. These were all people that he admired and that inspired him. Roy had watched the first team training and could imagine himself training alongside them. Once the games began, he rose to the challenge and used all his skills to control, pass, and create opportunities. Roy was the top goal scorer but the pressure to maintain the pace was beginning to take its toll. He struggled to breathe. Roy willed himself to play on and outrun the other lads and passed the ball forward for his team mate to take the fourth goal of the game. Roy stopped and reached down into his sock for the inhaler. He sucked on it hard before leaning forward and resting his hands on his knees.

"That's it," Roy thought as his breathing slowly became a little easier. *"I'm done."*

Roy fought off the tears that wanted to explode from his eye sockets as visions of his future as a professional footballer evaporated away.

The recruiters congratulated Roy on his skills and teamwork on the final day of the trial. However, they didn't believe that, due to his asthma, he could play out a full game so regrettably they were unable to offer him a place with Arsenal Football Club.

"I scored three of the four goals," Roy thought as he waited outside the ground for Costas. *"So that's it. Thanks to this asthma all my dreams of playing professional football are gone. What the hell am I going to do now?"*

Costas arrived and the huge smile on his face immediately fell away when he spotted Roy. Costas reached over and opened the door for him. Roy smiled weakly and got into the car. Costas checked his rear-view mirror before slowly driving away from the ground.

"I know and understand, Roy, that this is extremely difficult for you and you must be in a lot of pain right now," Costas said as he squeezed Roy's arm with his left hand. "You did your best and that is as much as anyone can ever do."

Roy pressed his lips together and nodded.

"Be proud of yourself for getting the trial," Costas said in an upbeat, positive, tone. "I'm proud of you Roy."

"Thank you Costas," Roy said as he battled to hold back tears.

"Do you want to talk about it?"

Roy shook his head.

"Okay, but when you do, don't hesitate to call me, alright, and I promise that I'll stop whatever I'm doing and give you time," Costas said.

"Thank you," Roy said as a single tear fell from the corner of his eye and slid down his cheek. He immediately wiped it away.

"Now don't you go giving up on football, alright?"

"I could never do that," Roy said. "I love the game."

"Good, just because you can't get to play at professional level doesn't mean that you shouldn't continue to enjoy playing football and being part of a team, "Costas said as they left Hertfordshire and entered London.

Costas drove through the Ledbury Estate and stopped by the block of flats Roy knew as home.

"Life is not a football trial where you pass or fail," Costas said as he turned to Roy. "It is a journey that you must grasp with both hands."

Roy listened intently.

"You are to move on from this Roy, by taking one step at a time," Costas said. "This crazy life that we are all living expands and contracts to an individual's courage and believe me, Roy Larner, you are one of the most courageous young men I know."

Roy couldn't answer for fear that he may cry.

"Never give up on anything that life throws your way," Costas said. "There will be continuous trials and errors, mostly errors, and believe me I know. Do not look at this experience as a failure because in the whole scheme of things it was just a lesson and life is all about learning."

Roy thanked Costas and got out of the car.

At home, with the bedroom door firmly closed, he covered his mouth with a pillow and allowed all the pent-up emotion and hurt out.

Chapter 10

In 1983 Roy's brother, Chris, moved out of the family home and he was able to move into his own room. Roy had taken some of his pocket money and purchased a Madonna poster featuring her iconic seductive pose which he put up on the wall to the right of his bed. Then directly over his bedside table he pinned an A4 glossy pic of Britain's favourite glamour model, Linda Lusardi, alongside a Millwall scarf.

Costas had given Roy the opportunity to work with him at the shop and the warehouse in Commercial Road at the weekend and on school holidays and was paying him a good wage. Costas would take Roy with him to meet suppliers, collect stock and then move it on to customers. They spent hours chatting about football and the future whilst on the move and while eating together at the cafés.

With his new found wealth, Roy would stop at the local newsagents every day and buy a copy of the Sun newspaper on his way to school.

Roy, Tony and Danny Eagle were now paying regulars at Millwall. The team manager, George Graham, had moved in and replaced players that had failed to prove themselves. The results were instant and dramatic with supporters witnessing Millwall pick up twenty seven points over twelve games. The excitement around the Den was euphoric as Millwall Football Club, under George Graham's leadership, was a team now finally capable of promotion.

However, Millwall Football Club continued to get dogged by bad publicity as fighting broke out at Tonbridge. The terrace battle involved over one hundred youths including visiting Chelsea fans from Tunbridge Wells.

Millwall Football Club was victorious with a 7-0 win.

Chapter 11

Wednesday March 13th 1985

A s Roy pulled his black Fred Perry Polo shirt with the gold motif over his head, *'Easy Lover'* by Philip Bailey & Phil Collins played on the radio. Roy checked out his reflection in the mirror before looking down to see how his new Adidas trainers looked.

"Today is going to be brilliant," Roy thought as he ran the comb through his hair. *"Millwall away, love it!"*

Millwall were playing away at the Kenilworth Stadium, Luton in the sixth round of the FA Cup.

Roy looked up at his giant wall poster of Madonna as *'Material Girl'* by Madonna played on the radio.

Roy continued to be a fan of Ska music but he couldn't take his eyes off Madonna's blatant interpretations of sexuality as she cavorted across the small screen while singing one great hit song after another. Madonna was, like so many young men, Roy's teenage fantasy figure.

Phyllis had left for work at the bank under the illusion that her son, Roy, was on his way to school. However he had returned shortly after she left to get changed out of his school uniform. Roy was bunking off school to attend the Millwall away game with his friends Tony and Simon.

Just as the chart's number one *'You Spin Me Round (Like a Record)'* by Dead or Alive began to play, Roy turned the radio off. He reached under his pillow and produced the tickets for the away game.

"Right, I'm all sorted," Roy thought as he closed the front door. *"Mum thinks I'm going to Tony Eagle's after school, having dinner and watching the football."*

Roy took a shot from his inhaler before bolting down the stairs where Tony and Simon were waiting.

"Have you got your ticket?" Simon said as Roy approached them.

Roy held it up with a huge grin spread right across his face.

"I am buzzing," Simon said as the three friends traipsed across the Ledbury Estate.

"I was reading this article the other day and they reckon the Den is the most intimidating ground in the country," Tony said as the lads climbed aboard the bus taking them to Kings Cross Station.

"You know why that is," Roy muttered.

"No, why?" Simon asked as he sat down.

"Because no one likes us and we don't care," Roy said with a broad smile.

Roy sat back in his seat and found himself remembering an incident on the estate a few years back:

"Here, on my head," Simon had called out as Roy raced towards the make-shift goal.

"Over!" Roy cried out as he chipped the ball over to Simon who netted it firmly between the lines.

"Yes!" Simon yelled, punching the air and running over and wrapping his arm around Roy's neck.

Roy dribbled the ball back to where the lads were playing.

"Oi!"

Roy turned to see a tall lad wearing skin tight blue Levi jeans, ox-blood high leg Dr Marten boots and a white Ben Sherman with blue braces. It was Stacks, a known Skinhead bully boy from across the estate.

"Oh no, this could get nasty," Roy thought as he stopped dead and placed his right foot on top of the ball.

"Pass the ball," Stacks called out, motioning him to kick it over.

"I've heard what you do," Roy thought as he stood firm. *"You ain't nicking our football."*

"Come on, pass it over," Stacks said in a firmer tone.

Roy looked at his friends, then at the ball and finally back at Stacks.

"No." Roy said.

"What did you say?" Stacks said, as his eyes widened.

"You heard me," Roy said calmly.

"Do you know who I am?" Stacks called out as he stomped over towards Roy.

Roy nodded and stood firm.

Stacks stopped just a few feet away and looked Roy up and down before smiling.

"Look, I'm not in the mood for beating up young kids today so just pass the ball," Stacks said with an evil snigger.

Roy maintained eye contact and slowly clenched both fists.

"If you want it, you'll have to go through me to get it," Roy said as he stepped forward in front of the ball.

"What, do you have a death wish or something?" Stacks said as he looked Roy up and down for a second time. "I've asked you nicely and now I'm telling you, matey, pass me the ball!"

"He's doing too much talking," Roy thought as he maintained eye contact with Stacks. *"If he was going to do something then it would have happened by now."*

Stacks took a short exaggerated step forward. Roy didn't flinch.

"Come on then," Roy thought as he clenched his fists tighter. *"I'm ready when you are."*

"What's your name?" Stacks said.

"Roy, Roy Larner."

"You've got guts, Roy, so today you've got lucky because I'm giving you a pass," Stacks said before pulling out a switchblade and holding it up for Roy to see.

Roy stood firm.

Stacks revealed a manic grin as he put the switchblade back into his pocket.

"See you around, Roy Larner," Stacks said before turning swiftly and walking away towards the chippie.

Roy had learnt from an early age on the Ledbury Estate that when kids back down to a bully, they don't ease up or go easy on them. The bullying only intensified and if unchallenged, it becomes a daily ritual. Roy had concluded, while still in single digits, that it was better to stand up for yourself and fight, even if meant getting a good hiding from a bigger kid.

"Penny for your thoughts," Simon said when he noticed Roy had been day dreaming.

"Well it's not football," Roy answered with a grin.

"Yeah, you're thinking about that American sort, Madonna," Tony said, making a sexy curvy shape with both hands.

"Can't blame him," Simon said. "I haven't been able to get her out of my head since seeing her in that 'Borderline' video.

"Oh yeah, I remember that one," Tony said with a chuckle.

"Roy's got a poster of her above his bed," Simon said.

"Yeah and that's about as close to getting Madonna in your bedroom as you'll ever get," Tony said with a laugh.

The bus stopped by Kings Cross train station and the three lads got off and bought return tickets to Luton. They wandered through the station and out onto the platform. The train was due to leave at 10.30am and the journey would take around one hour.

As Roy sat down in the train, a memory shot into his head of Costas sharing his wisdom a few days earlier:

"Roy, real men always give more than they take."

"I wonder what he meant by that?" Roy thought as he turned his head towards the window. *"Almost everyone I've ever known has taken more than they give. Obviously that doesn't include Mum, because she's the most selfless person I've ever known. However, most people are selfish and greedy but aren't they all only trying to survive and get by?"*

The train slowly pulled away out of Kings Cross.

"This is it!" Simon said as he punched the air. "We're on the move."

"Maybe Costas meant that some people's lives are so empty that they need more time, charity or empathy to fill the void, and a real man would give to that person because he can." Roy thought, smiling at his excited friends.

The train trundled up towards Bedfordshire when a smart young man in his early twenties sat by them.

"Alright lads?"

Roy nodded.

"Are you going to the game tonight?"

"Yeah, and you?" Roy said cautiously.

"I'm Terry Martin and Millwall through and through."

The lads smiled.

"You're early," Terry said.

"Yeah we bunked," Simon said before Roy interrupted him.

"Yeah, we're making a day of it," Roy said.

"And there was me thinking that you lads had all bunked off school," Terry said with wry grin.

"It'll be a big turnout tonight for sure," Terry said. "There is a hell of a lot more Millwall out there in the home counties that only turn up for important games and these are proper handy lads."

Roy had seen and knew of Millwall's Firm, 'The Treatment' and the 'Half Way Line' at the Den and hadn't considered there being any Millwall fans outside of New Cross and the surrounding areas.

"So are you with the firm?" Roy asked bluntly.

Terry smiled and shook his head.

"Millwall's top lads are the most notorious firm in the country with boxers, martial artists and seasoned armed forces lads in their ranks, and yet in their designer gear they just waltz straight by the authorities," Terry said with a chuckle. "No lads, I'm just a terrace Casual wanting to see his team win at Luton."

Football Casuals was a movement and fashion culture that superseded the 1970s bovver boy with his Skinhead haircut, boots and braces and designer, branded, clothing and smart trainers.

"Who are the Luton Lads?" Tony said.

"The MiG's," Terry said. "The lads call themselves 'Men in Gear' or MiG's because of their love for designer clobber."

"Are they a handy firm or what?" Tony said.

"Well they can have a row, but they're not in the same league as say the Headhunters, ICF, Yid Army or the Leeds Service crew,"

Terry said before lighting a cigarette and blowing the smoke towards the small opening in the train's window.

The train rolled into Luton. The platform was clear of police which was unusual for a Millwall away game even at 11.30am for an evening kick off.

"You lads have a good day and make sure that you mob up with the crews when they arrive," Terry said. "You don't want to get picked off in the side streets on your own."

"Yeah, will do. Be lucky," Tony said as he waved.

"He seemed like a nice enough fella," Roy thought as he handed over his ticket at the gate.

Roy, Simon and Terry spent the day walking around Luton town centre. They looked through the vinyl records at a local record shop before each buying a pasty from the bakers. By the middle of the afternoon Roy was acutely aware that a lot of Millwall were arriving. The police had a minor presence at each end of the High Street but the pathways were rapidly filling with loud, enthusiastic, supporters helping themselves to fruit from stall holders and newspapers from the front of newsagents.

The three lads watched as several lads slammed open an off-licence door and strutted out carrying trays of lager.

"Trouble is brewing," Roy thought as the thefts became increasingly brazen.

"Roy!"

Roy turned to see two lads, Lagging Del and Bazzer, who they all knew from the Den.

"Lagging Del," Roy called out as the two friends shook hands.

Del had earned his nickname because he always had a can of lager in his hand.

"Mate it's all happening here," Lagging Del said as he tore off cans of lager and handed them to Roy, Simon and Tony.

"Big numbers," Simon said.

"Yeah, but not all Millwall," Lagging Del said. "I've seen some of the Chelsea Combat 18 lot and Bazzer swears he spotted some Gooners (Arsenal supporters).

"What are they doing here?" Roy thought as he ripped the tin open and drank some of its contents. *"This is a Millwall game."*

"Are they here to take liberties?" Simon said.

Lagging Del shrugged his shoulders.

"I can't believe how small the police presence is," Lagging Del said before sipping thirstily at the can of lager. "A game like this would normally have old bill all over the place."

SMASH!

Roy and the lads turned to see a bunch of lads scarpering down the street having just put a shop window through.

Roy turned sharply when he heard the sound of tyres screeching. Burning tyre smoke was belching out of the rear arches of a Ford Capri as two lads were running in the road while trying to kick the car.

There was talk amongst fans that pubs and shops all over Luton had their windows put through and still the police presence was minor.

At 5.45pm the lads started making their way to the Kenilworth Stadium.

"Have you got tickets?" Lagging Del said.

"Yeah," Roy answered.

"We ain't," Lagging Del said with a husky smoker's laugh.

"The game's not being televised so there's no point plotting up in a pub," Roy said as they approached the stadium.

"We'll sit patiently until Millwall is properly mobbed up and we'll have it through the turnstiles," Lagging Del said.

Roy swallowed the last drop of lager in his tin before throwing it into a rubbish skip. Simon and Tony did the same.

"We might see you on the other side," Roy said.

"You can count on it," Lagging Del said before he and Bazzer turned away to join a mob of fifty plus lads.

Millwall Football Club had asked that the game be all-ticket only. The request was ignored.

At 7.00pm the vast Kenilworth stand, reserved for away supporters, was packed, with Millwall lads even perched on the scoreboard supports. The turnstiles had broken down and the Lion supporters were flooding the stadium in huge numbers. The Bedfordshire police were overrun as hundreds of lads scaled the fences in front of the stand before racing down the pitch towards the Oak Road end. Bottles, nuts, and bolts were thrown at the fleeing home supporters. Cries of pain filled the air as missiles found their targets.

Roy and the lads watched as the players from both teams came down the tunnel to warm up on the pitch. When they saw the rioters ripping up seats for weapons and tearing off towards the Bobbers stand, they rapidly disappeared back down the tunnel.

Moments later a message appeared on the stadium's electronic scoreboard.

"Look at that," Simon said, pointing to the scoreboard. "They're not going to start the game until everyone is back where they should be."

"Come on Millwall," Roy thought. *"We need to win this game."*

"It doesn't look like anyone is going anywhere," Tony said as he pointed towards the carnage in the main stand.

Finally George Graham, the newly appointed Millwall Manager, made an appeal over the loudspeaker. However, the rioting and violence continued until he appeared on the side lines and then slowly the Millwall lads returned to the stands.

With the aid of uniformed officers and dogs, the match began at 7.45pm with some Millwall lads watching from the floodlight pylons above the Bobbers' stand.

The referee blew his whistle and game began.

"Come on Millwall," Roy called out as Centre Forward Steve Lowell won his tackle and passed the ball forward.

The ball passed between Millwall and Luton with neither side taking a dominant position.

"Come on Lions," Roy thought as he scrutinized every pass. *"Make us proud!"*

"This looks like another nil-nil score with another replay," Simon said, shaking his head.

Fourteen minutes in and a mob of Millwall lads kicked off with broken up seats being lobbed at the home fans. The referee halted the match and ordered both teams off the pitch.

"We're not doing ourselves any favours here," Tony said as he stared down at the empty pitch.

"We could win this," Roy said. "With Steve Lowell and John Fashanu up front and a strong defence, we could dominate this game."

"At this rate we'll be leaving here for breakfast," Simon said.

Twenty five minutes later the referee led the players back out onto the pitch with Luton finding the courage to push forward.

"What the hell are we playing at?" Roy shrieked as he watched Luton's Brian Stein steam down the field, through Millwall's defence and put the ball clean into the back of the net.

The euphoric Luton fans yelled as their team took a 1-0 lead.

Half time came with both teams leaving the field and Luton maintaining the lead.

"They need a good talking to," Roy said. "We're a better team than this."

"Some you win and some you lose," Simon said as he shrugged his shoulders. "All part of being Millwall."

"I don't believe it has to be that way," Roy thought as he replayed the forward's play in his mind. *"We could have taken early control of the game. Luton was on the back foot and we played safe in the opening minutes and handed them that first goal on a plate."*

"It ain't over until the final whistle," Tony said. "We've done it before and we'll do it again."

The second half started with Luton taking the lead with strong passes.

"They've got us," Simon said.

"Give it a rest, Simon," Tony said.

"Alright lads."

Roy and the boys turned to see Lagging Del, holding a can of lager, and Bazzer.

"You got in then?" Roy said.

"Yeah me and about five thousand others," Lagging Del said with a hoarse chuckle. "Tell you what though lads, I don't think any of this lot have the stomach for a defeat. Mark my words, this is going to go off in epic proportions."

"We could still bring this round," Roy said as he turned back to the game.

"Come on, come on!" Roy thought as he watched the ball slip past Millwall again and again.

"There you go," Lagging Del said as he pointed towards hoards of uniformed police officers racing up the side lines.

"They've got dogs," Simon said.

"So what," Bazzer said. "If it comes near me I'll bite its throat out."

The police presence had amplified the atmosphere and with Millwall 1-0 down and the prospect of a defeat, tensions had heightened.

"It'll take more than a few plod to hold this lot back," Lagging Del said. "They're just skin and bone in a uniform and will bleed like everyone else."

Roy continued to watch the game but noticed that Les Sealey, the Luton goalie, had clutched his head and fallen to one knee.

"Someone must have lobbed something at him," Roy thought. *"Lagging Del is right, it feels like a tinder box of emotion in here and a defeat will light the fuse."*

The final whistle blew and Luton was victorious with a 1-0 score.

The fuse was lit and hundreds of Millwall lads stormed the pitch. Players from both teams and the referee, after a minor struggle, raced up the tunnel to safety. The Millwall firm marched on the Bobber's stand. Within seconds the dividing fence was torn down and seats torn up and broken down with the component parts being used as missiles to rain down on the police as they grouped together. With a single command, Millwall's lads were over the top and charging towards the police. Roy watched as one officer held up his hand as if ordering the attackers to halt. A series of left and right hooks followed by an almighty uppercut had the officer flat on his back and out cold.

"Like I said," Lagging Del said as he put his arm around Roy's shoulder. "Just skin and bone in a uniform. They go down like everyone else."

The officers were beaten back. One police dog leapt up to sink its teeth into one lad. The lad turned swiftly and delivered a killer right hander that sent the Alsatian police dog sprawling to the ground. As it clambered clumsily to get back on its feet the lad booted the dog in its rear, lifting the canine clean off the ground. The Millwall lad stood firm with fists clenched by his side. The officer turned and ran. The dog scrambled to its paws and bolted after the officer. With the visiting fans showing no signs of fear and battering all the police officers in their way, the police made a hasty retreat.

As one, the visiting ten thousand plus mob sang at the top of their voices while the police regrouped at the far end of the pitch.

"No one likes us

No one like us

No one likes us

We don't care

We are Millwall

Super Millwall

We are Millwall from the Den"

With batons drawn, the first wave of police officers ran back up the field brandishing their weapons. The two sides clashed with fists, boots and police batons flying. The police were beginning to get the better of the fighting when the lads pulled back as one, allowing a storm of broken up seats and metal piping to rain down on the armed officers. With the police in retreat for a second time, everything and anything that could be pulled, broken or just ripped off was sent hurtling down onto the police.

Roy, Simon and Tony watched from the stand as an unwritten policy of taking no prisoners saw the visiting fans battering officers that were trying to help their fallen colleagues.

"We should get out of here," Simon said as he looked down at his watch.

"Yeah, I told my mum that I was watching a game with you two," Roy said.

Roy and the lads left Lagging Del and Bazzer in the stadium and made their way back to the train station where they caught the train back to Kings Cross Station.

The ultra-violence at Luton continued with fighting in the town, windows being smashed and cars vandalised. There were eighty-one injuries sustained during the horrendous orgy of violence, of which over forty were police officers. There were thirty-one arrests while the carnage raged through the town of Luton. They were brought before the magistrate the following morning.

The Millwall Firms had cemented their position as one of the nation's most notorious Firms.

Chapter 12

"I've got some good news for you, Roy," Costas said as Phyllis handed him a cup of tea.

"Really?" Roy said as he perked up in the armchair.

"Yes," Costas said with a broad smile. "Rather than spend all your summer holidays hanging around the estate, my sister, who works with a recruitment agency, has managed to get you a summer job at Cable & Wireless in the post room.

In 1979 the Prime Minister of the Conservative party, Margaret Thatcher, began privatising the nationalised industries. A subsidiary of Cable & Wireless, Mercury Communications, was granted a licence for a UK telecommunications network to rival British Telecom.

"That's brilliant," Roy said as he visualised himself opening a weekly wage packet.

"Its good money too, very good money for a young man," Costas said with a wink.

Costas handed Roy a sheet of paper on which was written the start date, time, address and who he had to report to on arrival.

"Thank you," Roy said, glancing over at the wall clock. "Do you mind if I meet up with Simon, Tony and Danny? The Corona truck will be here soon."

"Roy, Costas has come to see you," Phyllis said as she sat down on the settee.

"Oh, okay," Roy said.

"Go on," Costas said before taking a sip of his tea. "I don't mind if your mum doesn't."

Phyllis placed her cup on the coffee table, reached into her handbag and pulled out a five-pound note.

"I need you to go to the chippy before 6.30 alright, and get the usual?"

"Sure, I can do that," Roy said as he leapt up from the chair and took the five pound note.

"You're a good boy, Roy," Phyllis said with a warm, loving smile.

"He certainly is," Costas said as he puffed up his chest and watched Roy disappear out of the door and down the hallway.

Roy spotted his friends standing by the road side along with dozens of other kids from around the estate waiting on the Corona man.

"Alright Roy?" Simon said as Roy joined the group.

"Yeah, where's Tony?" Roy said as he turned to Danny.

"He's not allowed out," Danny said with a cheeky grin.

"Why, what did he do?" Roy said.

"Mum has got the right hump with him," Danny continued. "She's only gone and walked past the toilet and Tony is practising what he calls his 'peeing marksmanship', and he's got the door wide open and standing right on the edge holding his dick and then letting it

112

shoot out towards the toilet bowl. Until today I was the house reigning champion but when Mum asked what he was doing, he lost control and peed on the floor and walls.

"Oh, that's not good," Roy said with a chuckle.

"It gets worse."

"What?" Roy said.

"He's only turned around and peed all over her new dress," Danny said with a pained expression on his face.

"No way," Roy said as the image flashed across his mind.

"Yeah and she went bat-shit barmy," Danny said. "She clumped him one and gave him a right telling off before sending him to his room with the threat of no fish and chips."

"No fish and chips!" Roy said.

"There is one up side though," Danny said with a chuckle.

"What's that?"

"I get to keep the title of long-distance peeing champion," Danny said, breaking out into a raucous laugh.

Roy told his friends about his summer job at Cable & Wireless.

"That's brilliant," Simon said. "You'll have loads of money."

Roy shrugged his shoulders and smiled.

"What do you think you'll do when you leave school?" Danny asked.

"I'm not sure," Roy replied. "As you know I wanted to be a professional footballer but that isn't going to happen now, and what with me losing time from school because of the asthma attacks, I may struggle with the end of year exams."

"I know what I'm going to be," Simon said.

"Yeah, what?" said Danny.

"I'm going to get myself an apprenticeship in a garage and fix up motors," Simon said.

"I didn't even know you liked cars," Roy said.

"I don't especially, but dad has a mate who runs a garage and he said it'll be a good job because people will always need cars and they'll always need fixing," Simon said.

"True," Danny said. "There's always broken down motors around the estate. You could make a fortune."

Simon's face lit up.

"Yeah, a nice pocket full of money to go out with on a Friday night," Simon said.

"Look at him," Danny said with a snigger. "He's imagining himself arm in arm with some good looking bird."

"I bet it's not just any girl though," Roy said as he winked to Danny.

"I don't know what you mean," Simon said, trying to disguise his grin.

"Go on, admit it," Roy said.

"Admit what?" Simon said.

114

"Will you tell him or will I?" Roy said.

There was a moment's pause as Roy and Danny waited for Simon to respond.

"Yeah alright, so I have a thing for Karen," Simon said finally.

"Karen?" Danny said with a quizzical expression.

"Yeah you know, Karen and Julie," Roy said.

Danny's eye lit up.

"You mean *the* Karen and Julie?"

Roy nodded.

"Mate they are both well out of your league," Danny said.

"Says who?" Simon retorted.

"Well they're both about twenty years old and you're what, fifteen?"

"Age is just a number," Simon said adamantly.

"Okay, so let's say that Karen is interested in a boy who is still at school. What do you think Mad Mickey, her biker boyfriend will have to say about it?"

"Nothing because it will be our secret," Simon said softly.

"Have you even spoken to her?" Danny said.

"He has," Roy said with a chuckle.

"Really?" Danny said as he stepped back with a look of surprise.

"Yeah he said 'Hello Karen' as she passed by the chippie two weeks ago," Roy said.

"Well that's it then," Danny said with chuckle. "It sounds like you're well and truly in there mate."

"You two just don't get it," Simon said with an exaggerated huff.

"Oh I think we do," Roy said. "She's the best looking girl on the estate, always wears short skirts with heels and she turns heads wherever she goes."

"In fairness," Danny said. "Julie does too. I mean they are two cracking looking girls but I just don't see it happening, Simon."

"You wait," Simon said as straightened himself up and pulled his shoulders back. "Once I'm working and have some money in my pocket, I'll be down the Sidmouth Arms and slowly but surely I will win Karen over with my good looks and boyish charm."

"What he means is he'll get her drunk and try his luck," Danny said.

The lads all laughed together.

"You can't blame me for dreaming, can you?" Simon said.

"Hey, it's important to aim high," Roy said. "Costas told me that."

"He's a good family friend, Costas, aint he?" Danny said.

"Yeah, he is," Roy said proudly.

"Always drives a quality motor, too," Danny said. "You never know, Simon, Costas could be one of your private customers once you've passed your apprenticeship."

"Yeah, working on BMWs and Jags would be cool." Simon said.

"Here he comes," Roy said as the Corona truck came into view.

"Oi, you lot," Danny said abruptly. "Get in line, behind us!"

The twenty plus boys and girls ranging in age from ten to fifteen shuffled together into a make shift line. The truck stopped and the driver jumped out of the cab and opened up the back.

"Right who is first?"

"That's would be us," Danny said as he stepped forward.

Roy bought a bottle of cream soda while Simon and Danny both had raspberryade.

"Don't forget now," the driver said as he handed Roy back his change. "Every bubble has passed its Fizzical."

The three lads laughed, then wandered down to the shops and sat down by the chippie.

"Costas reckons that the days of selling things like Corona and other stuff will all come to a stop as people are buying more from supermarkets," Roy said as he twisted open his bottle of Cream Soda.

"He could be right," Simon said. "My mum buys milk, meat and vegetables from the supermarket now. She reckons it saves time and money."

"I wonder what will happen to all the green grocers and butchers," Roy thought before taking a long swig from his bottle.

"Costas said that the only constant is change," Roy said finally as the memory popped into his head.

"I'm not sure that I like change," Danny said. "I kind of like things just as they are."

"I'm looking forward to being a grown up," Simon said. "We can go out, drink beer, get off with proper women, buy cars and even get our own homes."

"You're wishing your life away," Danny said.

"I'd like my own place one day," Roy said as he offered a swig to both Danny and Simon.

"Would you live around here?" Simon said.

"I would never move out of London," Roy said firmly.

"South London," Simon said with a grin.

"You mean South East London," Danny said as he raised his bottle of strawberryade.

Roy queued up for the family's Friday night treat of fish and chips. When he returned home he discovered that Costas had already left.

Once Roy had consumed his cod and chips he washed his hands and picked up the sheet of paper Costas had left for him. It read:

Post Room Manager Mr Thomas Hogben

Cable & Wireless

Theobalds Road

Holborn ECI

Monday 8.00am sharp!

Roy arrived at Theobalds Road at 7.45am and was immediately taken down to the post room and introduced to the manager, Mr Thomas Hogben.

"You must be Roy," Mr Hogben said, holding out his hand.

"Yes, I am sir," Roy replied.

"No need for the whole sir thing," Mr Hogben said, shaking Roy's hand. "In here you call me Tom but outside of the post room I am Mr Hogben, okay?"

"Yes sir, I mean Tom," Roy said with an awkward chuckle.

"Is this is your first job?" Tom asked.

"I am still at school but I've worked weekends and school holidays in a shop and a warehouse on the Commercial Road," Roy said.

"Good, good. I like to have a young man working alongside me who is not afraid of hard work," Tom said as he stepped backwards.

"Have you ever seen a post room before?"

Roy shook his head.

"No, but I'm keen to learn," Roy said.

Tom smiled.

"This place is the heart and central hub of a big, busy, business," Tom said. "It's where all the incoming and outgoing mail is processed and sorted for the departments."

"Okay," Roy said with a hint of excitement in his voice.

Tom pointed and explained that it was there that incoming mail was received, sorted and placed into pigeon-hole message boxes. He then pointed to a trolley which he called a mail cart and explained that a big part of Roy's job was to take the incoming mail, by trolley, to the various departments and then later in the afternoon collect all the mail due for posting out.

"I can do this, no sweat," Roy thought as he hung on every word Tom spoke.

"It can be stressful and demanding," Tom warned. "But you seem like the kind of young man that can rise to the challenge."

"I'll do my best," Roy said.

"That will be enough for me," Tom said as he walked Roy over to the sacks of incoming post.

Roy took to the working environment easily and very quickly got to know some of the people in each of the departments. Within a few days they were calling him by name and making light conversation. Roy enjoyed working.

On Friday afternoon Tom called Roy into his office and handed him a brown wage packet.

"More than a couple of departmental managers have called me to say how happy they have been with you, Roy, well done. You've made a sterling start.

"Thank you," Roy said as he glanced down at the pay packet.

"Mrs Roland in Marketing said that you hurried back to grab some important documents that had been missed and needed to be with a client."

"I sensed it was important," Roy said.

"It was, and there's a big contract resting on those proofs," Tom said. "It's been a long while since anyone actually phoned down here and thanked anyone for the work we do."

"I'm happy to help," Roy said.

"Refreshing," Tom said with a broad grin.

"Mr Collins said that you breezed into finance like a breath of fresh air, introducing yourself as 'Roy Larner, I'm new to the job but excited and looking forward to working with you'."

"Costas always said that it was important to be yourself," Roy said as he fumbled with the wage packet.

"Costas?" Tom said.

"Yes, he's a good family friend," Roy said.

"Well you've made a damn good start, now go on home and enjoy your weekend," Tom said as he sat back in his black leather desk chair. "See you bright and early on Monday."

"Thanks Tom," Roy said as he turned towards the office door. "You have a good weekend too."

Once Roy was out of the building, he turned to a brick wall and looked left and right, before opening the wage packet stuffed with ten- and five-pound notes.

"Wow, this is real money and a lot of it," Roy thought as he counted out three hundred pounds. *"I've never even seen this much money before except when I've been out buying stock with Costas. This is all mine, I earned it and the people I work with like me."*

Once Roy was back home on the Ledbury Estate he put on a smart pair of jeans, an Ellesse polo shirt and his new Adidas trainers that Costas had got for him.

"You look like a proper grown up now," Roy muttered to himself while holding up a wad of notes and checking out his reflection in the mirror.

"Are you off out?" Phyllis called out from the kitchen.

"Yes Mum," Roy replied as he ran the comb through his hair. "I'm meeting Simon, Danny and Tony."

"You're not playing football are you?"

"No, we might go to the community centre and play snooker," Roy said with a smile.

"Well, have a good time and don't be too late," Phyllis called out as Roy headed towards the front door.

"I won't," Roy said as he closed the front door firmly behind him.

"There will be no snooker at the community centre tonight," Roy thought as he strutted confidently down the stairs. *"We're going to try and get into the Sidmouth Arms."*

Having money that he had earned in his pocket made Roy feel a strong sense of achievement. He had been genuinely touched by Tom's comments and the nice things his work colleagues had said about him.

Roy spotted his friends standing a few feet away from the pub door.

The Sidmouth Arms is located at the intersection between Bird in Bush Road and Commercial Road Peckham, London SE15 and is a popular boozer with residents from the Ledbury Estate and surrounding areas. It had a name for being a hard pub with a reputation for violence. Roy had heard many stories about incidents between friends and families on the estate breaking out into violent brawls after a few beers. His understanding was that it was, generally, a friendly pub for locals but outsiders were made to feel unwelcome. Roy had heard about an alleged undercover police officer, who, with his short back and sides haircut and shiny shoes attempted to buy a pint of shandy in the pub on a Saturday night. The word had gone around the pub quickly and two lads stood either side of the undercover police officer. When the officer refused to be intimidated by them, one of the lads took his drink and drank every drop before belching loudly and suggesting that either he left now or in an ambulance later. The suspected undercover police officer left. While the locals looked upon the Sidmouth Arms as a 'proper pub', outside visitors believed it to be intimidating.

"Well, are we going in or what?" Roy said as he looked over to the door.

"I'm skint," Simon said.

"I'll get you a pint," Roy said.

"I'm up for it," Danny said.

"Yeah, me too," Tony said.

Roy took a deep breath.

"Right, let's do this then," Roy said as he turned swiftly on his heels and marched towards the pub door.

As Roy led them into the smoky bar he turned briefly to the jukebox where he saw Karen and Julie reading through the playlist while *'Jump (For My Love)'* by the Pointer Sisters played.

Roy and the lads nodded to people they knew and recognised from around the estate before settling at an empty table.

"Right, quids in," Roy said as he held out his hand while Danny and Tony both placed a one pound note in his hand.

"I'll have to owe you," Simon said.

"You can get it next time," Roy said before turning sharply and strutting over to the bar.

"Come on Roy, just keep a straight face and look like the working man you are," Roy thought as he held up a one-pound note to attract a passing barmaid.

"Oh no, I recognise her," Roy thought as the barmaid approached him. *"She lives in our block."*

The barmaid looked Roy up and down.

"I know you, don't I?"

"Yeah," Roy said with a broad, awkward, smile. "We live in the same block. You're Lyn, right, and you have a younger brother Billy that plays the guitar?"

"That's right and you are?"

"Roy," Roy said as he held out his hand.

Lyn shook his hand.

Lyn had magma red hair that crashed and spiralled over her shoulders. Her jade green eyes sparkled under the pub's bright lights.

"What can I get you, Roy?" Lyn said with a grin.

Roy looked briefly toward her heart shaped lips. They were succulent, sultry and velvet soft.

"Four pints of lager, please and have one yourself," Roy said as he reached into his pocket for more money.

"Tennents, okay?"

Roy nodded.

"You're a big spender then?" Lyn said as she took a tall straight glass down from the shelf and began pouring his drink.

"No, it's just my first week at work and I'm out having a drink to celebrate it with friends," Roy said.

"I'm not telling you that it's just a summer job and I'm still at school though," Roy thought as he reached over to sip the first pint she placed on a tray.

"Well that's a very nice thing to do and if it's okay with you I'll have half a lager with a lemonade top."

"Sure," Roy said as she placed the last pint on the tray.

He handed over the money and Lyn gave him back his change.

"You have a good evening," Lyn said before lowering her voice. "I would keep out the way of Jim the landlord for a while."

"Oh, okay," Roy said as he picked up the tray.

"Don't worry, I'll square it with him," Lyn said with a friendly wink.

Roy carried the tray back to the table like he was carrying a trophy.

"No problems at the bar then?" Danny said.

"Nah, none at all. It was a breeze," Roy said with his tongue firmly in his cheek.

"Have you seen who is at the jukebox?" Danny said as he turned to Simon.

'Relax' by Frankie Goes to Hollywood was playing when all the lads turned around to see Karen in her short, beige coloured, Ra-Ra skirt with matching knee length leather boots and a brown top that accentuated her curves.

"She is stunning," Simon muttered.

"Yeah and I'm sure that you, me and every red blooded bloke in the pub thinks the same," Danny said as he cast his eyes over her voluptuous curves.

The lads watched as Julie, with her sunrise gold hair and burnt orange Ra-Ra skirt, joined Karen.

"I'd settle for some of that," Tony said as he watched Julie glide effortlessly across the pub.

"I wonder what they're talking about," Simon said as he watched the girls giggle while pointing down at the playlist.

"What record to play next," Roy thought as he took a sip of his lager.

"Maybe a little bird has told Karen that you fancy her," Danny said with a chuckle.

Simon beamed.

"Do you think?"

"No!" Danny and Simon said together.

"Mark my words, lads, I will get to have my wicked way with Karen," Simon said as he reached for his beer. "It's just a matter of time."

"Dreaming or fantasising doesn't count," Roy said with a laugh.

"I promise I'll get further than you will with Madonna or Linda Lusardi," Simon said defiantly.

"Maybe, maybe not," Roy said.

"If you get bored of your Madonna or Linda Lusardi posters, we'll have them," Danny said.

"Yeah, in a heartbeat," Tony said as *'Smalltown Boy'* by Bronski Beat began to play.

The lads stayed until closing time and had managed to put away two pints of Tennents lager each and were all feeling a little tipsy. Simon had the lads in fits of laughter when he looked up from their table and said 'Hello' to Karen as she passed on her way to the ladies. Mad Mick arrived with a couple of his biker friends just before closing. Roy overheard them saying that they were riding up to Chelsea Bridge.

***

The three weeks passed quickly at Cable & Wireless. On Roy's final day Tom announced his plans to retire and that he had put a good word in for Roy to run the post room if he wanted the job. Roy knew that the acute asthma attacks had forced him to miss time from school, and would affect his chances of gaining any decent qualifications. He liked the job and the people he worked with and the money was ten times more than an apprentice was getting, so he decided to leave school immediately and start working at Cable and Wireless on a six-month trial.

The pace of life changed rapidly once Roy was working full time. His weekly routine very quickly became Friday night out with the lads at the Sidmouth Arms, follow Millwall on a Saturday, back in the pub with his growing circle of football mates, playing for the Sidmouth Arms football team on a Sunday morning and then into the pub until gone closing time.

Despite Roy's increased circle of friends and good money in his pocket, he remained extremely shy around girls.

At Cable & Wireless Roy excelled at every task and job placed before him. He developed trust and friendships with the people he worked with and was offered, eighteen months later, the opportunity to transfer to the in-house print business. Roy accepted the role and was now working four days each week with Fridays spent studying for his City & Guilds 524 Print Management qualification at The London College of Print at The Elephant & Castle.

Roy took his driving test three times. He failed the first time and had an automatic fail the second time around as he had been suffering from an asthma attack. However, he passed his third test before his 18th birthday by requesting a 'cancellation' test. Costas was extremely proud of his achievement and bought him his first car... a light blue Volkswagen Beetle 1303S.

Photographs

Roy and his partner Tracy Johnson

The Apple & Pears pub

Roy & former work mates Andrew Goblin, Dave Keen & Andrew Percival

Roy & his brother Paul with mates in Athens

Roy at home on the Ledbury Estate Peckham

Roy with his comics and a copy of The Sun Newspaper

Roy helping out Costas at his warehouse

Roy with dad, Costas

Harry Chapman tweeted: Quote of the year. Article written by Matt Wilkinson.

Roy in the pram with dad (Lee) & brothers Chris and Brian

Roy, Phyllis (mum) & brothers Chris and Brian

Roy on Clacton Beach

Cyprus with mates from the Sidmouth Arms

Rhodes with mates from the Sidmouth Arms

The Ledbury Estate Peckham by Mum's house

Mum, Phyllis, has lived here on the Ledbury Estate for 50 years

Roy with Ashley Walker & John Gibbons just before the New Den opened

The Cable & Wireless football team

Millwall away game with a few mates

Roy with his daughter, Freya's, dogs Cooper & Toby

My good friend, Aiden, left me this book 'Learn to Run' while in hospital

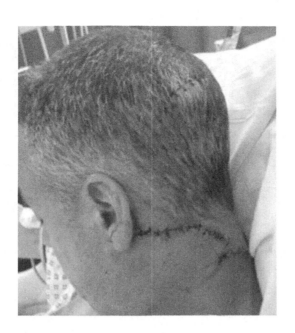

A few of the injuries after the London Bridge attack

Good Morning Britain with Piers Morgan & Bradley Walsh

Photo by Mick Lowe
Left to right: Champ Lloyd Honeyghun, Lord Davies of Abersoch CBE, Mark Prince, Tony Davis, Roy Larner, Scott Welch (Chair of WBC Cares UK),Barry McGuigan and John Conteh.

Roy receiving a medal from the WBC

The Newspaper interview my mum, Phyllis, did for a newspaper

Charles Bronson very kindly sent me a couple of paintings

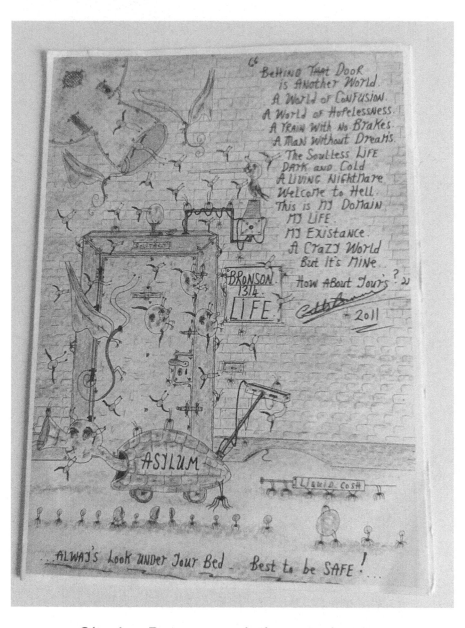

Charles Bronson painting number two

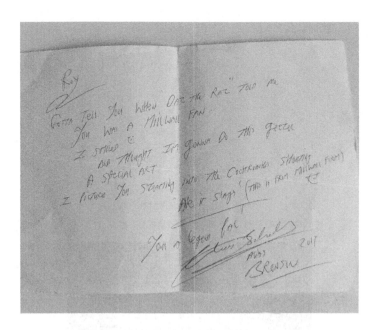

Charles Bronson message

Roy's feature in the Evening Standard Magazine

Calum Beaton
Cuffley, ENG, United Kingdom

👥 31
Supporters

Petition to Theresa May MP, Sadiq Khan

London Bridge terror attack hero Roy Larner to get George Cross

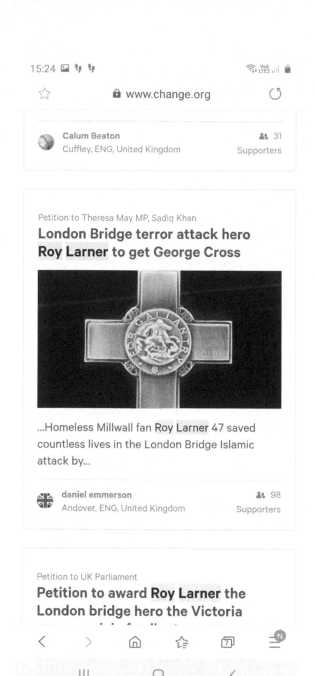

...Homeless Millwall fan Roy Larner 47 saved countless lives in the London Bridge Islamic attack by...

daniel emmerson
Andover, ENG, United Kingdom

👥 98
Supporters

Petition to UK Parliament

Petition to award Roy Larner the London bridge hero the Victoria

One of many petitions for Roy to receive the George Medal

*Going back to The Black & Blue to finish my drink
after being released from hospital*

*Roy with staff at the Black & Blue after being
released from Hospital*

Spiderman wanted a photo

Roy with BBC Reporter Lucy Grey

Plaque revealed on June 5th 2022

My beautiful daughter, Freya

Roy having a quiet pint

*Portrait of Roy by Bill Barrett on show at Phillips 30
Berkley Square*

Fearless Hero's sing: The Lion of London

Arthur Kitchener sings: The Lion of London Bridge

Podcast with Paul Stansby

Roy with Rhiaz Khan

Roy with Jane Jacobs & Friends before a game at the Stanley Arms

Front Cover of the Millwall Magazine with Grant Merrill, Darren Kelly & Gerard Vowels

Roy & Dean Rinaldi his friend and ghostwriter

Roy & Tracy Johnson

Chapter 13

"**R**oy, have we had the Bank delivery?"

Roy understood the term 'Bank' was common print jargon for lightweight paper, typically less than 60gsm and most commonly used in typewriting.

"It came in this morning, Colin," Roy replied as he stood over his print machine. "I put it away in the stores and left the delivery note on your desk."

"Thanks," Colin replied. "I'm popping out for half an hour."

"Okay, I've got this," Roy said as Colin stepped out of the print room.

Colin was the print manager and had been with Cable & Wireless for over twenty years. He was always fair and reasonable. They had a good working relationship. When urgent jobs were thrust upon the department, Roy would always volunteer to stay and see the job through with Colin and the team. Colin treated his lads as family. It was an atmosphere that Roy excelled in.

Cable & Wireless launched the Mercury 21 mobile phone on September 7th 1993. Roy and his friend Andrew were so excited that they got theirs on the day of the launch. The cost was almost five hundred pounds but the company provided interest free terms with monthly payments deducted from their salaries. The package included free phone calls between 7.00pm and 7.00am.

With the machine in full operation, Roy picked up his copy of the Sun Newspaper to double check what horses were running at the Cheltenham Gold Cup. He had overheard a couple of lads at the Sidmouth Arms talking about the race and a horse's name resonated with him.

"I think I need to put a couple of quid on Charter Party," Roy thought as he read the form.

Roy looked down at his watch.

"If I shoot across to the bookies now I'll be back in twenty minutes," Roy thought as placed his newspaper on the table. *"Yeah, I'll do it now because we have a match at lunch time."*

Roy played for the inter-company team most lunch times and was averaging between four and five goals every game.

Roy double checked his machine and then left it running while he bolted off across the road to the William Hill betting shop. As he filled out his betting slip, he had to take a second look as a girl with lavish, long star-flame gold hair that wreathed her moon shaped face served a customer.

"Wow!" Roy thought as he put his pen down on the shelf. *"She is stunning."*

Roy found himself watching how she interacted with the elderly customers.

"She's just lovely!" Roy thought as he glanced at her alluring galaxy-blue eyes. *"I need to say something, anything."*

Roy understood that shyness was not a simple black and white issue but a continuum and he had learnt not to be too hard on himself.

"Why can't I just slip over there, bold as brass, and just be me like I am around Dario's sister, Melissa?" Roy thought as he watched the beautiful blonde take the next bet. *"I want to say something but it can't be another blunder."*

Roy looked down at the betting slip, then his watch and then the blonde.

Suddenly, without any warning, the blonde looked up at Roy and smiled.

"She noticed me," Roy thought. *"What do I do now?"*

The blonde looked up again and held Roy's gaze for a few moments.

"I think she likes me," Roy thought as he looked down at his betting slip for the second time. *"Right, Roy, now it's time to man-up and get over there and say hello."*

Roy strolled over to the counter and placed his betting slip before her.

The blonde girl looked up and Roy couldn't help thinking that her puffy lips were sumptuous, sensuous and kiss-inspiring.

"Hi," Roy said.

"Hello," the blonde said, looking down at Roy's betting slip. "This is for the Cheltenham Gold Cup."

"Yes," Roy said before pausing for a millisecond. "The horse just jumped out at me so I thought I'd have a flutter."

"Well, I wish you luck then," the blonde said with a smile.

"I'm Roy." Roy said as he looked down briefly at her perfectly manicured nails.

"Hello Roy, I'm Jean, Jean Jones," Jean said with a bewitching, angelic smile.

"Damn, you are breath taking," Roy thought as he returned the smile.

"I've never seen you in here before," Roy said.

"I was working part time and now they've moved me to full time," Jean said.

"What time do you go for lunch?"

"I can't believe I've just said that," Roy thought as he squeezed his fingers tightly into a fist. *"What if I've blown it?"*

Jean chuckled.

"I stop for lunch at 1.00pm," Jean said while maintaining eye contact.

"Me too," Roy said.

"Gone on, go for it!" Roy thought.

"Do you fancy meeting up for a drink?" Roy said gingerly.

"That would be nice," Jean said.

"Do you know the Lady Ottoline in Northington Street by the tube station?" Roy said with a hint of excitement in his voice.

Jean nodded.

"I pass it every day on my way here," Jean said with a broad smile.

"Great, I'll meet you there," Roy said.

"Okay," Jean said before handing Roy his betting slip and change.

"Yes!" Roy thought before turning away from Jean and leaving the bookies. *"I did it and Jean is beautiful"*

Roy called the lads at work and told them that he couldn't play that day because he was meeting a girl for lunch.

"I love the sound of that," Roy said as he checked his reflection in the mirror. *"I'm meeting a girl for lunch."*

Jean arrived at the pub just a few moments after Roy. They found a seat by the open fireplace and Roy went to the bar to order chicken in a basket for them both, a pint of lager for him and a gin & tonic for Jean.

"Whereabouts do you live?" Roy said before popping a hot chip into his mouth.

"Canning Town," Jean replied, dipping her chicken strip into the sweet chilli sauce.

"Oh no, not a West Ham fan, are you?" Roy said with a chuckle.

"So, what's wrong with West Ham?" Jean said before taking a nibble of her chicken strip.

"How long have you got?" Roy said with a cheeky smile.

"You'll be telling me that you're a Millwall supporter next," Jean said, slowly shaking her head.

"That would be me," Roy said proudly.

"Well that's not a good start is it?" Jean said before taking a larger bite of the chicken strip.

"A good start..." Roy thought. *"She must like me then."*

"I'm only kidding," Roy said.

"Do you actually know why there is such a fierce rivalry between West Ham and Millwall?" Jean said as she reached for her gin and tonic.

"Sure," Roy said before taking a sip of his pint. "This kind of stuff gets handed down from one generation to another."

"So it's a bitter rivalry then?"

Roy took an exaggerated intake of breath.

"The rivalry is more intense than that of any of the other English clubs," Roy said. "It dates back decades to when Millwall Athletic and Thames Ironworks, both East End clubs, were just a few miles apart and the bulk of their support came from Dockers. Millwall moved to the south of the river and I suppose it was then that the rivalry started when they started competing for business. If you fast forward to the Krays in East London and the Richardsons in South London during the sixties, it has just kind of stuck."

"Sounds silly to me," Jean said.

"When you say it out loud like that I suppose it does," Roy said.

"I need to get off the subject of football," Roy thought. *"I don't want to blow this."*

"Are you one of those hooligans, Roy?" Jean said as she sat back in her chair and waited for his answer.

"My passion is Millwall Football Club and my love is for football," Roy said. "Yes I go to home and away games as a loyal supporter of the club but I do not look for trouble, ever, but if it finds me I will not leave my friends, under any circumstances, or run away."

Roy managed to turn to the conversation around to music and he shared his love of travelling up to Dean Street Records in Soho to buy imported records. Jean was impressed when he said that he had over three hundred records in his collection. As the clock got closer to 2.00pm, Roy gathered up the courage to ask Jean out on a date and…. she accepted.

Roy and Jean became boyfriend and girlfriend and stayed in a fun, no strings, relationship for eighteen months. However, with Millwall defying all the odds and winning promotion to the first division for the first time in their history, Roy made a personal commitment to attend every home and away game.

Eventually the relationship ran its course and Jean told Roy that it was over and that she had met someone else. Roy had wanted to be angry, but he knew in his heart that football was his first love and when he sat down and really thought about it, he was pleased for Jean and they remained friends.

Despite a defeat against their arch rivals, West Ham, Millwall finished one place above Manchester United, the pre-season favourites. Roy had become increasingly confident and with money in his pocket, he was hanging out with the older lads and so graduated from the Sidmouth Arms to the Kentish Drovers in Peckham, a pub predominantly used by Millwall lads. Pre-match drinks for home games were always at the Bramcote Arms in Bramcote Grove and then straight back, win or lose, for a session. Roy transferred to the Bramcote Arms pub football team and played on Sunday mornings.

August 27th 1988

Roy met up with Simon, Tony and Dave Keene for the away game at Aston Villa. They travelled up to Birmingham from London with a huge number of supporters. The game started on time and Millwall took an early lead with forward Tony Cascarino putting the first goal of the match away. Roy and the thousands of Millwall supporters were euphoric and cheered for over ten minutes. The final score was 2-2

September 1988 was a brilliant month for the Lions as Roy and his friends witnessed Millwall beat Derby 1-0, Charlton Athletic 3-0, Everton 2-1 and finally had a 2-2 draw against Norwich.

October started well with a 3-2 win over QPR, a 0-0 draw at Coventry City and a 2-2 draw against Nottingham Forest. They were defeated 4-2 at Middlesbrough.

On the 5th of November the police, anticipating a repeat of the 1985 riots, lined the train platforms and streets before Millwall played Luton. Millwall were victorious with a 3-1 win.

Millwall supporters travelled to Liverpool in big numbers for the game at the Anfield stadium. Roy and his friends only witnessed a couple of minor incidents outside the stadium but the day ended with a 1-1 draw. It was considered by all as a result and a great day out.

The game against West Ham on December 3rd, despite the rivalry, went off without any major incidents and there were only reports of a few minor skirmishes taking place away from the ground. Millwall were defeated 1-0.

Roy and his friends were thrilled to be travelling the country to support Millwall against Arsenal, Tottenham, Newcastle, Southampton and Nottingham Forest.

The year ended with Millwall Football Club playing thirty-eight games. They won fourteen, drew eleven and lost thirteen.

In February 1989, the 'Battle of Highbury' was committed to the Terrace Casuals' history books. Roy had travelled with his friends and thousands of Millwall supporters the short distance to Islington. It was to be a big game and Millwall supporters from all over the South-East turned out in big numbers. The local pubs were rammed packed before the game. The Plimsoll arms and the Arsenal Tavern in Blackstock Road erupted into an orgy of violence with glasses and bottles being thrown and seats being torn up before the heavy bar stools were thrown through the windows. Both pubs were trashed in minutes. The five hundred plus specially trained police officers were unable to contain the terrifying violence when Arsenal Gooners and Millwall's Lions clashed again on the streets.

Roy and twelve thousand Millwall supporters were crammed together into Arsenal's Clock End. However, a mobbed up firm of Lions had got into Arsenal's North End. Once the referee blew his whistle there was a ferocious roar of 'MILLWALL!' in the North End followed by an almighty brawl. The lads in the Clock End cheered as they witnessed the carnage. Police tried to restore order but were pelted with coins.

Arsenal won the game 2-0.

Rumour had it that some of the visiting supporters had managed to steal the clock from the Clock End.

Chapter 14

England faced Montenegro at Wembley during 1993. Roy and England's supporters willed the players on to get the one extra point to qualify for the World Cup 94. They succeeded.

"We did it Roy," Mark, his mate from printing college, said.

"What a result," Roy said as he punched the air. "Rotterdam here we come."

"Are you going then?" Mark said as the lads left the stadium.

"Mate, I can't think of anything better than travelling overseas with all your mates to cheer the English players on," Roy said before taking a deep suck on his inhaler. "You are coming, aren't you?"

"I hope so," Mark said.

"Hope so, what do you mean hope?" Roy said as he patted his friend on the back. "This is England in Europe and if we get just one more point then we're on for the US 94.

"Yeah I know, but what with me getting married I can't just up and go like before," Mark said.

Mark had recently married a lovely Swedish girl.

"Just ask her mate," Roy said. "There's no need to lie or to be deceitful. Just tell her how important it is for you to see England win in Rotterdam. I'm sure she'll understand," Roy said.

"I'll try," Mark said.

"Do you fancy a drink before going home?" Roy said.

The friends stopped off for a drink at a pub down the Old Kent Road.

"What you having?"

"Lager," Roy said before acknowledging people he knew from Millwall around the pub.

"I'm right buzzed up over Rotterdam," Roy said before taking a sip from his drink. "It's an incredible feeling when you win a game overseas."

"Yeah, yeah I get the picture," Mark said as the two friends bumped glasses. "I'll be there."

"Can I leave it to you to get the tickets?" Roy said.

"Yeah, sure, how many?"

"Three," Roy said.

"Three?"

"Yeah, me, you and Dave Keene," Roy said.

"No problem, I'll get it sorted," Mark said

The barman placed their second pints on the bar.

"Mark," Roy said quietly.

"What, mate?"

"What's it like being married?"

Mark smiled before taking a long sip of his beer.

166

"It wasn't top of my list of things to do," Mark said before taking another long sip. "We had been together for a while and everything was, well you know, going great and then random people from around the family started asking me when I was getting married."

Roy nodded.

"Well that got me wondering," Mark said before placing his drink on the bar. "Should I get married? But then I thought, 'well isn't just living together enough?'"

"I did chat about it with a couple of trusted mates and they were of the opinion that marriage wasn't compulsory to having a long and happy relationship," Mark said.

"That makes sense," Roy said. "I know loads of people who live together and are not married."

"Yeah, but that doesn't mean that there aren't good reasons to get married," Mark said. "I came to the conclusion that tying the knot would be right because our relationship is built on trust and love."

"That's a good thing," Roy said as he reached for his drink.

"It was never about religious beliefs or values," Mark said.

"You clearly have solid foundations," Roy said.

Mark nodded.

"I suppose, once I had come to terms with my thoughts, I wanted something that was firm, you know a solid bond underpinned with a ring and sworn declaration," Mark said.

"I'm pleased for you mate."

"Cheers," Mark said as he raised his glass.

"I can understand wanting a long term commitment with someone special," Roy said. "I suppose it sets the foundation for a family."

"Yeah, we have been talking about it," Mark said. "I think I'd like our own little boy or girl or even one of each."

"I'll drink to that," Roy said.

"I would never slide into getting married just because we had been together a long time. Let's face it, if you're already unhappy then putting a ring on a girl's finger isn't going to change anything," Mark said.

"Fair point," Roy said. "Your mum and dad like her though, don't they?"

"They love her to bits mate, but even that didn't factor into my reasons for finally proposing," Mark said. "I suppose the bottom line, for me, was love and trust and I had that in abundance. Why do you ask, Roy, have you been seeing someone?"

"No, nothing like that," Roy said with a chuckle. "I've had a couple of long term relationships but they were never anything that either of us took seriously. They had their life, interests and commitments and I had my football."

"What happened?"

"They ran their course and they moved on to someone else," Roy said as he shrugged his shoulders.

"Oh, monkey branching," Mark said, shaking his head.

"What's that then?" Roy said as he motioned the barman to bring them two fresh pints.

"It's when a woman doesn't let go of one branch before they have a firm grip on another," Mark said.

"That's a bit harsh," Roy thought.

"It wasn't like that," Roy said. "In fact I've stayed good friends with them both and honestly, Mark, I'm genuinely happy for them. They were both right. What we had would never have stood the test of time and they were braver than me by calling it a day."

"Fair play mate," Mark said. "Are you interested, you know, have you got your eye on someone a bit special?"

"I'm not about to tell you that I'm still a little bit shy around girls," Roy thought.

"No, I'm happy with my work, my mates at the pub and going to football," Roy said as the barman placed two pints on the bar. "That said, if I were to meet someone special, like you have, then who knows."

***

October 12th 1993. The day before the big game at Feyenoord Stadium in Rotterdam.

Roy, Mark and Dave Keene took the underground tube to Liverpool Street Station where they bought tickets to Felixstow for the overnight ferry to Rotterdam. When they arrived they found themselves surrounded by hundreds of England fans travelling away for the big game. Once on board they joined the travelling England fans.

***

"Tommy. Hello mate, how are you?" Roy said as he shook hands with his old friend from the Ledbury Estate.

"Hello Roy," Tommy said with a big, mischievous, grin. "How the hell are you?"

"Good mate and you?"

"Fair to middling at best mate," Tommy said.

"Tommy, this is Mark and Dave," Roy said and the lads all shook hands.

"Alright boys."

"I thought you were away," Roy said quietly.

"I was mate," Tommy replied. "The old bill stitched me up good and proper."

"What, for real?" Roy said with a wry grin.

"Yes mate, they stuck me down with a robbery charge in Lewisham and I wasn't even in London," Tommy said as he shook his head.

"Couldn't you prove it?" Roy said.

"They reckoned the evidence was inadmissible in court and weighed me off for three years," Tommy said through gritted teeth. "They lied through their teeth mate. It was all I could do to just sit there in the dock. Every muscle in my body wanted to clamber over the dock and batter the officers into telling the truth which was... I'm innocent of all charges."

"What happened?"

170

"I was shipped off to Pentonville. The girlfriend hung around for about a month and then I lost my flat because there were no mortgage payments being made and my plastering business went down the toilet because I wasn't there to manage the contracts," Tommy said.

"Tommy, mate, I'm gutted for you," Roy said.

"My brief stayed on the case and eventually, eighteen months later, the conviction was overturned. The copper that fitted me up had a string of cases fall apart and so they took a good look at mine," Tommy said. "I made them pay though."

"Good for you," Roy said.

"No amount of money properly compensates for the loss of eighteen months, my home and a business I'd spent years building," Tommy said.

"What about the bird?" Mark said.

"She was long gone. Upgraded to some bloke in the city who traded commodities or something," Tommy said.

"Harsh mate," Mark said.

"Hey, things are on the up though," Tommy said as his smile brightened.

"I put myself about to all my old contacts and slowly but surely I started picking up work. It's not quite where it was before they put me away, but another twelve months or so and it will be," Tommy said as he puffed out his chest.

"You can't trust some of these old bill," Mark said as he opened a tin of lager. "Do you remember when they had undercover old bill in Millwall, West Ham and Chelsea?"

"I remember that," Dave said.

"Yeah, well all those trials collapsed because of the fabricated evidence," Mark said. "I have this theory, right?"

"What's that?" Roy said as he winked at Dave.

"I reckon that a big chunk of the old bill are made up of kids that were bullied at school and so they joined up to wear a uniform and were then given the power to do pretty much what they like to get even and deliver results," Mark said. "Not all the old bill, but I bet there's plenty in the ranks who would be nothing more than a shopping centre security guard if the recruitment was done properly."

"I don't think you're wrong," Tommy said. "I met plenty of people inside who reckon they were innocent."

"They all say that though don't they?" Dave said.

"Believe me lads there are plenty of working class boys and men locked away for crimes they didn't commit because we're easy and believable targets."

"It's pretty scary when you think about it," Roy said.

"Anyway that was yesterday and now it's onwards and upwards," Tommy said. "I've just taken delivery of a Porsche 911 Turbo 3.6 Coupe and I've got this cracking little Thai bird on the firm."

"A Thai?" Mark said as his eyes lit up.

"Yes mate," Tommy said with a broad grin. "After being locked away I needed some time out in the sunshine and so I booked a ticket to Phuket. Lads you have to believe me when I tell you that those Thai birds are something else with their petite slender figures, long shiny black hair and large almond eyes."

"Yeah," Dave said

Tommy nodded.

"Nice soft, delicate feminine features and golden tanned skin," Tommy said. "The birds out there in Thailand knock spots off what's available back here in the UK. I have to tell you when I think about the ex and what I had to put up with, my Thai girl, Achara, is a breath of fresh air."

"How do you mean?" Mark said.

"Maybe it's just me but don't you think that some birds are becoming increasingly masculine like?" Tommy said. "I was in the pub a few weeks back with the lads and there were these birds at the bar, covered in tattoos, sinking lager like it was going out of fashion and then they started belching, and I mean with the mouth wide open and roaring like something from the Jurassic period. It was nasty, proper nasty."

"The same could be said about a few people at the Den," Roy said. "We all know lads that can act like animals."

"Fair point," Tommy said.

"I'd rather have a spirited London girl with attitude and something about her," Roy thought as he sipped his beer.

"So is Achara here permanently?" Dave said.

173

"No chance," Tommy said with a raucous laugh. "Once the six months visa is up she'll be going home. I was clear and upfront with her right from the start."

"I always fancied Thailand," Mark said with a sigh.

"I bet you did," Roy said as he patted his friend on the back.

"No really," Mark said defensively. "I've often thought it would a nice country to visit."

"It is," Tommy said. "You wouldn't want to live there, but a couple of months will certainly breathe new life into you for sure. I met a couple of lads that had fallen for some tanned beauty and stayed, but then that's when it all changes."

"In what way?" Mark said.

"I don't want to generalise but Thai girls do look upon westerners as their personal entertainment centres. They all think we're loaded and expect to be wined, dined and entertained daily," Tommy said. "But lads, if you do go there and find yourself in the company of Thai girls, be very, very wary because they can fall for you within days and just when you're thinking 'this is nice' they're already naming the children, so leaving can become extremely difficult. That's why I was completely upfront with Achara."

"Mark's happily married to a nice Swedish girl, aren't you mate?" Roy said.

"Yeah, yeah of course, but it's always interesting to hear about other cultures," Mark said.

"Look, Roy, lads, I've just seen an old pal of mine so I'll catch you later," Tommy said as he shook Roy's hand.

"You look after yourself," Roy said as he watched his friend saunter over to a bunch of lads

"Nice fella," Roy said. "A proper grafter too. That fella will work around the clock to get whatever contract he's on done on time."

"It ain't right that the old bill can fit a person up and when discovered gloss it over with a 'miscarriage of justice' and just walk away," Mark said. "I feel for the bloke."

"Roy Larner, you old reprobate!"

Roy turned sharply to see a Chelsea lad he knew.

"How the hell are you mate?" Franklin said

"Good mate and happy to be on my way to watch England beat the Dutch in their own stadium," Roy said as he shook Franklin's hand.

"Are that lot with you Chelsea boys?" Roy said as he nodded towards a group of men wearing blue jeans and black leather bomber jackets.

"That's embarrassing mate," Franklin said.

"What do you mean, embarrassing?" Mark said as he tore the ring off his beer can.

"They call themselves Combat 18," Franklin said quietly.

"What's that then, a Firm within a Firm?" Dave said as he reached for a tin of lager.

Franklin shook his head.

"They're some Neo-Nazi group that wants to create a whites only Britain," Franklin said.

"What the hell has that got to do with football?" Mark said before taking several large gulps of his beer.

"Some geezer called Charlie started talking with Chelsea's top boys," Franklin said.

"You mean the Headhunters?" Dave said.

"Yeah," Franklin said. "He managed to persuade a bunch of them to join Combat 18."

"How on earth do they think they can create a whites only Britain?" Roy said. "I've got black mates who were born here, so they are British."

"All I know is that they have a political arm seeking power and Combat 18 is the muscle," Franklin said. "They want to ship all non-whites back to Africa, Asia and the Middle-East, either alive or in body bags. They're not fussed either way."

"That will never happen," Roy said.

"This Charlie, the bloke that runs it, seems pretty determined and by the sounds of it he's well connected," Franklin said before taking a sip of his beer. "They don't only have it in for non-whites, because they want to execute all queers and white race mixers."

"Radical is an understatement," Roy thought as he sipped his beer.

"That's some list," Mark said.

"It goes on," Franklin said with an exaggerated sigh. "They want to weed out all the Jews in any kind of powerful position and execute all those that have used their power and influence to damage the white race. Those that are left are to be thrown into concentration camps."

"It sounds like the kind of thing Adolf Hitler did," Roy said.

Franklin nodded his head emphatically.

"The numbers 18 are Adolf Hitler's initials. 1 for A and 8 for H," Franklin said.

"You seem to know a lot about it," Roy said.

"Me and my mate, Billy Warman, have been going to Chelsea since we were both kids at school," Franklin said. "Billy was handy, you know, he had an extremely short fuse and if tested would go way beyond your traditional tear up. Back in 91 we were playing Villa and their firm, 'Villa Hardcore', decided that they wanted to have some and Billy was in there with boots and fists flying and he's copped hold of this one black fella who had been strutting about like he was some kind of kingpin and given him a proper hiding, and I mean blood, guts and broken teeth. It was proper nasty. The top boys have seen him in action and pulled him into the Firm and that's when this Charlie geezer has recruited him into Combat 18."

"So you weren't tempted to follow your mate?" Mark said.

Franklin shook his head.

"Billy did his best sales job on me, which is why I know so much, but for me it's all about football and I don't sign up to any of the right wing political stuff they're selling," Franklin said.

"Do you still see Billy?" Dave said as he tore off a beer and handed it to Franklin.

"Only in passing," Franklin said

"I couldn't see Millwall's top boys entertaining any of that Combat 18 lark," Mark said.

"I wouldn't be so sure," Franklin said as he ripped the can open. "You Millwall boys are on the Isle of Dogs, right?"

Roy, Mark and Dave all nodded.

"It's a working-class area and didn't you have some kind of protest with the slogan 'Rights for Whites'?"

"I remember that," Roy said. "Some bloke called John Stoner was set about by a group of Asian lads and his grandfather led the three hundred odd people march."

"Wasn't that the BNP?" Mark said.

Roy shook his head.

"No, his grandfather condemned the BNP," Roy said.

"All I'm saying lads, is that these people are dangerous," Franklin said. "I don't mean football tear up type dangerous. I mean take you outside and cut your throat in broad daylight type dangerous."

"It comes back to where we started then," Roy said bluntly. "What are they doing here?"

"Recruitment," Franklin muttered.

"Recruitment," Dave said.

"Billy reckoned that it would only be a question of time before they infiltrated London's top firms. He said that Millwall and West Ham were on their list."

"Oi Franklin, over here," a young lad with an England flag wrapped around his shoulders called out. "This mug has just put a tenner down saying that he can drink a tin of lager in three seconds."

"Three seconds," Mark muttered.

"Yeah, I'll be right there," Franklin replied. "Catch you later. If not, see you in Rotterdam."

"Take care," Roy said as the lads watched Franklin go back to his mates.

"Hold up," Mark called out before turning to Roy and Dave. "If that mug can do a tin in three seconds then I'll put down fifty quid that I'll do six tins in twenty five seconds or less."

"Don't get too pissed up mate, we've got Rotterdam yet," Dave Keene said.

"No problem," Mark said. "I'll see you later."

"We should take the tickets off him, just in case," Roy said.

"Nah, Mark's alright. I've seen him put away a lot more than that," Dave said.

The seven hour overnight journey from Felixstowe to Amsterdam passed quickly with lads drinking lager, chatting and generally having fun and joking about. As the ferry docked Roy and Dave set about trying to find Mark.

"Franklin," Roy called out.

Franklin turned back and smiled.

"Yes mate."

"Have you seen Mark?"

"Your mate Mark?"

"Yeah," Roy said anxiously.

"Roy he was with a right rowdy lot, proper pissed up," Franklin said.

"On or off the ferry?" Roy persisted.

"Off it mate," Franklin said.

"Cheers, Roy said before waving over for Dave to join him. "Catch you later."

"We're proper stuffed," Dave said. "Mark's got the tickets."

"Tell me something I don't know," Roy said as he peered anxiously from left to right.

"I've got a tattoo on my John Thomas," Dave said with a chuckle.

"What?" Roy said.

"You said to tell you something you didn't know," Dave said with a short laugh.

"Mate, we ain't got time for jokes," Roy said, still scanning the army of England fans marching down into Rotterdam.

"Tommy," Roy called out when he saw his friend.

"Roy, what's up mate?" Tommy said.

"We've lost Mark," Roy said as Tommy joined him.

"Roy, he's been nicked," Tommy said.

"You're joking!" Roy said.

Tommy shook his head.

"He was well out of it and started giving this copper some grief and I mean proper gobbing off," Tommy said. "The next thing he's being marched off."

"How long ago?" Roy said desperately.

"Five minutes at the most," Tommy said. "He was dragged off that way."

Roy followed his pointed finger to a side road along the docks.

"Cheers," Roy said as he bolted away with Dave close behind him.

"You have our tickets Mark, and you better not have ruined it for us," Roy thought as he pushed past the supporters. *"Seen you!"*

Mark had been handcuffed and was sitting on the kerb alongside two other lads.

"Mark, you mug!" Roy said as he approached him.

"Yeah, I know," Mark slurred.

"Stand back!" the police officer said.

"Do you still have the tickets?" Roy mouthed silently.

Mark nodded.

Roy nodded to Dave and then faced the police officer.

Instinctively Dave walked over to the police officer and engaged him in conversation. Meanwhile Roy crouched down and removed the tickets from Mark's jacket pocket.

"I'm gutted," Mark whispered.

"I suspect you'll be the first of many," Roy thought.

"We'll be at the YMCA if you get out," Roy said.

Mark nodded and then lowered his head.

With the tickets safely in his pocket, Roy and Dave wandered down into Rotterdam's city centre to get a drink.

Roy and Dave joined a group of lads and plotted up in a bar. The atmosphere around the streets was tense with small groups of police officers in full riot gear and holding batons.

"This could go off," Dave said as he handed Roy a pint.

"There are way too many serious people here for the police to be pushing and shoving indiscriminately," Roy said.

"You ain't wrong," came a voice behind Roy.

Roy turned to see a couple of lads he knew from the Den.

"Vince, Ozzie, how are you?" Roy said. "What are you drinking?"

"We've just got one in, you're alright," Vince said. "Where's your mate, Mark?"

"Nicked for mouthing off," Roy said.

Vince shook his head.

"We were talking to a bunch of lads that got in a couple of days ago and went up to Utrecht," Vince said as he stroked his chin. "They took the train in this morning and the old bill, seeing that they were England fans, gave them a good kicking."

"What for?" Dave said.

"Nothing, just for being England supporters," Vince said.

"It's all part of being a travelling England supporter," Ozzie said. "The press would love to have the public believe that we're the ones kicking off, when nine times out of ten an opposing firm rocks up looking for trouble or the old bill get a bit handy with a few too many lads and a line is drawn in the sand, old bill or not."

"Maybe Mark's theory about British old bill is the same the world over," Dave said.

"What's that?" Vince said.

"Mark has this theory that a lot of old bill were bullied kids at school," Dave said before sipping his beer.

"I'd go along with that," Vince said.

"Me too," Ozzie said. "I've seen them run when the mobs turn."

"I saw it at Luton in 1985," Roy thought as memories of uniformed police officers running flat out, with dogs, away from the supporters entered his mind.

"Have you lads got tickets?"

Roy nodded.

"Have you?" Roy asked.

Vince shook his head.

"Nah, we tried but came anyway," Vince said.

"We might be able to pick some up outside the stadium," Ozzie said.

"Chances are, with over five hundred of us, they'll just put us into the stadium anyway," Vince said as he shrugged his shoulders. "Let's face it, they'd be better off knowing where we all are."

As the evening progressed there were stories being told around the pub of clashes between England fans and the riot police in the city.

"You can't just batter people and think you'll walk away from it," Ozzie said.

"Do you know what makes me laugh?" Vince said. "The newspapers would have you believe that your average England supporter is a nutcase, you know some kind of psychopath, and yet the fearless dominance and cold heartedness displayed by some officers in dangerous or emotionally charged situations and are prone to use excessive force and disregard any rules. I reckon they get off on brutality while hiding behind a uniform and an institution."

***

At closing time Roy and Dave headed to the YMCA.

Match Day:

The police, dressed in full riot gear, lined the city to the Feyenoord Stadium. Roy and Dave had joined the forty eight thousand supporters approaching the ground.

"Did you see that?" Dave said, pointing out a single officer smacking an English supporter with his baton.

Roy nodded.

"Yet another example of excessive force by a police officer to maintain control," Roy thought as he carried on walking towards the stadium.

"They reckon over eight hundred of us have been arrested," Dave said. "Apparently they've brought in some kind of bylaws which pretty much means that the police can do whatever they want.

Roy had heard stories of English supporters being dragged out of bars and given a good kicking on the streets. He knew that there were plenty of naughty lads about, but the police and the Dutch hooligan fans were getting away with murder.

Once inside the ground, England fans were told that they were unable to buy alcohol. However the Dutch fans were buying beer on the opposite side of the segregation fences and were goading English supporters. Roy and Dave were bundled into the double decker stands behind the away goal with the other five thousand England supporters. The atmosphere was raw, gritty, loud and tribal.

Roy could feel his heart pounding as the England squad ran onto the pitch.

"Come on England!" Roy chanted along with the thousands of other loyal supporters.

The referee blew the whistle and the game was on. The Dutch dominated the opening minutes and when Frank Rijkaard's goal was disallowed as offside, the first half ended 0-0.

Roy and Dave heavily debated the game with the surrounding supporters during the half-time break.

The second half was away with the fans chanting David Platt's name as he ran towards the goal. The anticipation of a goal and putting England ahead was almost euphoric until Ronald Koeman pulled David Platt down at the edge of the box.

"That was right out of order!" Roy yelled out.

"Low life cheat," Dave hissed through gritted teeth. "That goal would have seen us on our way to New York next year."

"Koeman knew that," Roy muttered.

The fans roared and began celebrating as the referee ran towards the penalty area.

"This is it," Dave cried out as he hugged Roy. "World Cup here we come!"

The referee gave a free kick and not a penalty.

"You're joking," Roy muttered. "That was a penalty all day long and Koeman didn't even get a red card!"

The referee blew the whistle and the Dutch illegally charged down England's free kick and the referee let it slide. Erwin Koeman, Ronald's younger brother, then kicked Paul Parker right in the family jewels and walked away without a booking.

"This is fixed," Dave grumbled.

"What, are you blind, ref?" Roy yelled out.

Then Koeman hurled the ball, after a questionable free kick re-take decision, into the top corner.

"No!" Roy cried out.

The Dutch fans erupted with deafening cheers of joy. Smoke flares were let off as the atmosphere turned hostile. With Bergkamp slamming the second goal away, the Dutch had secured their place to play in America.

'Always Look on the Bright Side of Life' pounded through the speakers at full volume.

"That just adds insult to injury," Roy said as they left the stadium.

The Dutch had urinated into their plastic beer glasses and thrown them over the segregation fence at the English fans. Officers pounded their batons into their open hands as they held the fans back from leaving the stadium.

"They're taunting us," Dave said. "Look at them all big and brave in their riot gear and the full weight of the Dutch law behind them."

"It's like they want the England supporters to respond," Roy thought as he looked up to see a bunch of lads setting fire to the seats at the top of the stadium.

Roy and the England fans were finally released from the stadium where they were being goaded by some of the Dutch officers.

Roy was feeling angry, shocked and disillusioned by the 2-0 result.

"Either the ref is a complete numpty or the game was rigged," Roy thought as he walked through the city to the train station to catch the train to Amsterdam.

The police, anticipating problems, had closed down half of Amsterdam.

Roy and Dave joined the hundreds of fans returning to England where they were met by the press, photographers, film crews and the police.

Chapter 15

Roy had been chatting with his football mates at work. They had just won the BT League

"We're outsourcing most of the print now and the future isn't looking good," Colin Niles, the print manager said.

"So where does that leave us?" Roy asked.

"I've managed to secure us both a job in Milton Keynes," Colin said with a half-smile.

"Milton Keynes? Where is that?" Roy said as the shock of moving away from his home dawned on him.

"It's in Bedfordshire," Colin said as he shrugged his shoulders. "It can't be more than thirty miles away.

Roy found himself thinking about the inter-company football they had played in Porthcurno, Cornwall and the London games. He had even signed up for the cricket team but they were slaughtered by the West Indian lads. However, they had won every football tournament over the last five years

"I don't suppose I've got a choice," Roy said.

"Look, the company will give you a ten thousand pound relocation allowance to make the move easier. Roy, you could even buy a house," Colin said.

"Buy my own house," Roy thought. *"Interesting."*

***

Roy accepted the role and shared the news with Costas.

"I've got a place in Stotfold," Costas said. "It's not a million miles away from Milton Keynes.

"Really?" Roy said with a hint of shock.

"Sure, you can stay there for free.

"Right let's think this through," Roy thought. *"I'll be working Monday, Tuesday, and Wednesday, college at the Elephant & Castle on Thursday and with a bit of wiggle room I could stay in London on Friday to have a pint with my mates, Millwall home or away on Saturday and play football on the Sunday before having a session to finish the weekend off, sweet."*

Roy accepted Costas' offer and moved to the new premises in Milton Keynes. Colin had worked things so that Roy could stay at the London office on the Friday. Despite the move going well, Roy missed living in London, Millwall and his mates.

"There you go," Costas said as he handed Roy a tin of beer.

Costas had a warehouse in Stotfold where he kept the bulk of his stock.

They talked about the move and how Roy was feeling, and as always, Costas would turn it all around with some well-chosen words of advice.

"You've always been good to me and the family," Roy said before sipping his drink.

"That's what family friends do," Costas said.

"Yeah, but you've always been there and helped Mum out with money when Dad was away and you've always been especially good to me," Roy said.

Costas took a long sip from his drink.

"I like your mum, she's a nice lady, and she works hard for her family," Costas said.

"My friends would often ask me as a kid why you were so good to me," Roy said. "But I never asked why.

There was a moment's silence.

"Costas, why are you so good to me?"

Costas took another small sip of his drink and then placed the can on the coffee table.

"Do you know what you're asking me?" Costas said.

Roy nodded.

"Okay," Costas said. "I think that I may be your dad."

"What?" Roy cried out as he spilt his drink down his shirt.

"Look, I don't know for sure, but I think I'm your dad," Costas said.

"What, you and Mum...?"

Costas nodded.

"Your dad was away and well, it just kind of happened," Costas said.

"Away, you mean banged up in prison?"

Costas nodded awkwardly.

"What does Mum think?" Roy said as he wiped his shirt.

"She thinks it too," Costas said.

Roy leaned forward and put his head in his hands while he thought.

"So my brothers are not my brothers then?" Roy said.

"Of course they are, Roy," Costas said reassuringly. "You share the same mother."

"I don't know what to say," Roy said as his life and everything Costas had helped him with flashed before him.

"It may be that I'm not," Costas said. "I am more than willing to take a blood test though. It will confirm it one way or another."

Roy shot up from his chair.

"I'm tired and I'm going to bed," Roy said as he stomped across the living room and down the hallway.

"I'm here when you're ready to talk," Costas called after him.

Roy tore off his shirt and threw it onto the floor before falling down face first on the bed. He was completely devastated.

"I don't believe this," Roy thought as the tears streamed from his eyes. "I don't bloody well believe this! The life I thought I had has been a complete lie and here I am twenty odd years old and have only just found out. I feel completely destroyed and lied to by everyone I love and care about."

Roy wiped the tears from his face.

"Who else knows this?" Roy thought. *"Does Dad know? Does Dad know what... that he's not my dad?"*

Roy turned over and looked up at the ceiling.

"Maybe I always had my suspicions," Roy thought. *"No one else I know has a family friend anything like Costas. So what happens now? Does my dad blank me and Mum becomes angry at me for finding out and what about my brothers? Is that it now, do they turn on me?"*

Roy shook his head slowly.

"Costas is a good man and he's been a damn good family friend," Roy thought. *"I will not turn on him, never, but what do I do now?"*

Roy turned to the window where he saw the clouds move slowly across the full moon.

"I feel so angry but I don't know who to be angry at!" Roy thought as he clenched and unclenched his fists. *"What does this make me?"*

As the clouds passed by Roy turned away to face the bedroom wall.

"I don't want to hurt my dad, even if he knows or even suspects about Costas, so I can't talk to him about it. I wouldn't even know where to start with Mum and I don't want to lose my brothers. so what do I do?" Roy thought as his eyes welled up. *"Right, you just carry on as normal, Roy! Stop blubbering about what has happened and just get on with everything as if nothing has changed. Do not get a blood test and just say nothing to anybody. It's not anyone's business but mine."*

Roy rolled over onto his back.

"That's what I'm going to do and that way everything goes on as it did before," Roy thought. *"I'll say no more to Costas and close him down quickly if he tries to talk about it again. This is the right thing to do or risk blowing everything apart including Costas' own family."*

It was well after 4.00am before Roy finally fell asleep.

Chapter 16

"That's the way to do it," Roy said as he walked towards the Foresters Pub in Bermondsey with a group of older Millwall boys. "A solid 2-0 win with Tim Cahill and Paul Ifill smashing the ball clean into the back of the net."

Roy had just watched Millwall play Ipswich at the Den. It had been a good game with a turnout of just over eight thousand and the boys were buzzing. As they entered the busy pub, *'Unleash the Dragon'* by Sisqo was playing on the jukebox.

The landlord recognised them immediately and had one of the barmaids start pouring pints. The boys downed the first pints in seconds and it was then that Roy caught a glimpse of the new barmaid. He left his pint on the bar, took a deep breath, and then strolled down the bar to where she was pouring a pint.

"I've not seen you in here before," Roy said with a broad grin. "I'm Roy, Roy Larner."

"Nice to meet you Roy," the barmaid said as she poured the pint of lager. "I'm Tracy, Tracy Wicks."

"I could be in here?" Roy thought as he ran his eyes over her slim, svelte, figure.

"I could make this my local knowing that you'd be here, Tracy," Roy said.

"Why did you say that? It was so bloody corny!" Roy thought as he looked at the way her swirls of caramel brown hair toppled over her shoulders.

"Oh you must be the sweet talker of the bunch then," Tracy said as she placed the pint on the bar and started pouring the second.

"I just thought you were very pretty and wanted to say hello, that's all," Roy said.

Tracy stopped pouring the drink and looked up into his eyes.

"Really? Or are you just trying to sweet talk your way into another notch on your bed post?" Tracey said with her eyes firmly fixed on Roy's.

"I just like you," Roy said.

"Good," Tracy said as she continued to pour the drink. "You'll want to take me out on Friday then."

"Yes, definitely," Roy said with a smile that spanned the entire width of his face.

"You'll want my telephone number then?"

Roy nodded.

***

The following day Roy called Tracy from work and they agreed to meet at the Foresters Pub on the Friday for a swift drink before venturing off down to the Old Kent Road. They got along extremely well. Tracy's forwardness made building the relationship easier and Roy felt very comfortable around her. The relationship blossomed, with Tracy introducing Roy to her two children, Ricky and Jade.

Winning Ricky over had been easy by taking him to football training, but he had to work hard to win Jade's trust and affection.

In 2001 Tracy had been feeling sick. It was a familiar feeling, so she took a pregnancy test. It was positive. Both Roy and Tracy were overjoyed at the prospect of becoming parents. Throughout the pregnancy the happy couple would refer to the unborn baby as 'Little One'.

"I've decided that I want a pool birth for Little One," Tracy said as she snuggled up to Roy on the sofa. "I want a natural, un-medicated, labour."

"Are you sure?" Roy said

"I'm sure," Tracy said.

"Then a pool birth you will have for our Little One," Roy said as he squeezed Tracy's shoulders.

The nine months passed quickly and Tracy's waters broke. She phoned the hospital and told them that her contractions were regular, strong and approximately five minutes apart and lasting for around sixty seconds.

Roy was excited and almost overwhelmed at the thought of becoming a dad. He believed it would give purpose to his life and would make him a better, more responsible, person.

Tracy began to gather a bag together, with Roy's help. They were ready and off to the hospital within minutes. Roy had been plagued with anxiety about whether the birth would go smoothly and had spent hours imagining what Little One would look like. He wanted, more than anything, to be supportive of Tracy and Little One throughout the pregnancy.

Tracy had explained to Roy that because Little One was not her first baby, the birth could happen very quickly and preparation was everything. Roy and Tracy arrived at the hospital in good time. She handed over her notes to the nurse at the maternity unit admissions desk. Roy was told to take a seat while Tracy was led into a labour ward where she was asked to change into a loose fitting hospital gown.

Roy joined her and the midwife in the delivery room. He sat and watched as the midwife took Tracy's pulse, temperature and blood pressure. She felt Tracy's abdomen to check Little One's position.

Roy's heart was racing. He was excited, anxious and had more energy than he could physically use up in the delivery room. When Tracy told the midwife that she was having a contraction she did an internal examination to find out how much her cervix had opened. Roy spotted a blue ball in the far corner of the room amongst the bean bags, mats and easy chairs.

The midwife helped Tracy step into the birth pool and the warm water.

Roy strolled over to the ball and brought it back to where he had been sitting. He placed the ball on the floor and began to roll it around with his feet.

As the birth progressed Roy found himself rolling the ball around faster and passing it back and forth between his feet. The Midwife looked up and scowled.

"Stop that now or you'll be removed!"

"Yes, of course," Roy said as he pushed the ball under his chair. "I'm sorry, it's just that I'm so nervous and excited about becoming a dad."

When Tracy yelled out that Little One was coming, Roy jumped to his feet. He called out words of encouragement.

"Something is wrong!" Tracy cried out as Little One was born.

Roy could see that the midwife was worried and called out for a doctor.

Little One was covered in blood but had dark areas covering her skin. The Midwife cleaned Little One over and over but the dark marks remained.

"Why are they not coming off?" Tracy called out.

"What is happening to my Little One?" Roy thought.

"Do you have a name for your baby girl?" The Midwife said as the doctor checked over Little One.

Roy eventually broke the silence.

"We came to an agreement," Roy said whilst looking at the doctor examining his daughter. "If it's a little boy then I get to name him, but as she is a little girl, Tracy gets to choose the name."

"Freya," Tracy called out. "Our daughter's name is Freya."

Freya was kept in the hospital for tests. Everyone had been stumped by the marks on her skin. Eventually an expert diagnosed Freya with having an acute case of 'CMN' or Congenital Melanocytic Nevi and a 'cleft palate'.

Both Roy and Tracy were upset, confused and broken as they asked themselves and the universe why their Little One had been made to suffer.

The symptoms of CMN are the presence of moles on the skin from birth, and range in colour from brown to black. Whilst they are painless, they had covered a great deal of baby Freya's body. The hospital staff were magnificent throughout the countless operations that Freya had to endure. It had been heart breaking for both Roy and Tracy and particularly tough on Freya.

In 2003 the printing was outsourced and Roy was made redundant, which added pressure to their relationship. As they pushed Freya in her pushchair, people would stop, point or stare. Roy was always quick with a firm, blunt, challenge. It was an incredibly emotional time for the family.

Freya would constantly shock both Roy and Tracy with her bravery, determination and tenacity. With the aid of a speech therapist Freya was talking normally and the operations on the CMN were making good solid progress.

Roy continued to follow Millwall but only at the occasional home game.

The years of hurt, anger, arguments and emotional pressure took its toll and in 2016, after a serious conversation with Tracy, it was concluded that it was best for Little One if Roy left the family home and returned to his mum's home on the Ledbury Estate Peckham.

Roy understood, but was devastated that he and Tracy were finished. He wanted to try and make up and become a family again but the feelings that were once there were now gone.

Roy loved his daughter and was immensely proud of Freya who had very quickly become a 'little mummy's girl'. She had surrounded herself with a great set of friends and was excelling at secondary school. During one of their meet-ups, she told Roy how she planned to leave school and go on to university so that she could become a nurse and help people. It was all Roy could do to hold back the tears as an overwhelming sense of pride washed over his entire body.

It had been an incredibly tough year on all the family, but Roy had been struggling more than he had previously. His world had fallen apart and even meeting up with old football mates for drinks only masked his sadness for a short time.

Chapter 17

Roy strode through Borough Market with his hands in his pockets. He was deep in thought.

"Roy, is that you?"

Roy turned to see, Jenny Waller, a friend he hadn't seen in a while. She had coral black hair that flowed and toppled over her shoulders and she had a warm, friendly, smile.

"Hello Jenny," Roy said with a broad grin. "You're looking well. How have you been?"

"I'm okay," Jenny said. "What about you? I haven't seen you in ages."

Roy took a deep breath.

"Are you still with Tracy?"

"No, we finished a while ago," Roy said with a sigh.

Roy explained briefly some of the stress and trauma that both he and Tracy had endured and how it had affected their relationship.

"I'm really sorry to hear that," Jenny said.

"Tracy and I still get on okay and I adore my daughter, Freya. I'm just so proud of her," Roy said with a sincere, joyful, smile.

"Where are you living now?"

"It's not the best of situations if I'm brutally honest," Roy said shrugging his shoulders. "I'm not working and jobs are hard to find, so I've been living back at Mum's on the Ledbury Estate."

"Work is hard to come by for everyone so don't beat yourself up," Jenny said. "It can't be easy living back at your mum's."

"I'm at rock bottom mentally and physically, Jenny, but I can't tell you that," Roy thought. *"I'm not thinking straight and the weight of all that has been going on has me feeling like my whole life is spinning out of control."*

"She's nearly eighty years old and the last thing she wants right now Is me, a grown man, coming and going," Roy said. "To be honest I don't think it's good for either of us. However, I'm staying upbeat and positive that a job will come along and I'll get my own place."

Jenny stepped back and paused for a few moments.

"Do you want to stay at my place?"

"Your place?" Roy answered with a quizzical expression.

"Yeah, I have a two bedroom flat just a few minutes from here by London Bridge," Jenny said. "My son, Aiden, is three and he still likes to come in and sleep with his mum."

"Am I hearing right?" Roy thought. *"Is Jenny offering me a place to stay?"*

"Really?" Roy said as his eyes lit up.

"Yeah, why not? We're friends, right?" Jenny said with a smile.

"Yeah, I know," Roy said. "Sorry, I'm just a bit taken back."

"Roy, you can stay at my place until you find your own home," Jenny said.

"I can't believe what I'm hearing," Roy thought.

"Jenny, I don't know what to say," Roy said.

"Say yes and then go home and thank your mum for allowing you to stay, grab your bags and get yourself over to here," Jenny said as she scribbled her address on a yellow post-it note and handed it to him.

"Thank you, Jenny, thank you so much," Roy thought.

"This is brilliant, Jenny," Roy said as he took the post-it note. "I really appreciate this."

Jenny looked down at her watch.

"I need to get going," Jenny said as she handed Roy a front door key. "Let yourself in and get settled and I'll see you later."

Roy looked down at the key.

"What an incredibly kind thing to do," Roy thought. *"You see, Roy Larner, life is not all doom and gloom and there are still some damn good people out there, and Jenny Waller is one of them."*

"Thank you," Roy said just as Jenny turned swiftly on her heels and walked away.

"This will take so much pressure off Mum," Roy thought as he made his way back to the Ledbury Estate. *"She really doesn't need me or anyone invading her space at her age. Thank you Jenny for this opportunity to get my life back on track."*

Roy packed his bags, thanked Phyllis, and got himself over to Jenny's flat. He settled in and was quickly accepted by Aiden. The Borough Market was only a few minutes from Jenny's flat and Roy knew several people there, including Nelson who managed the Market Porter pub.

Chapter 18

The Stanley Arms Pub, Southwark Park Road, London SE16. Saturday May 20th 2017.

The English Football League (EFL) one division final between Millwall and Bradford City was to be played at Wembley Stadium to determine the third and final team to gain promotion to the EFL Championship.

Roy had arrived along with fifty plus jubilant Millwall Supporters just after 7.00am.

"I am buzzing," Harry said as he shook Roy's hand. "You're looking well son."

"Life is feeling pretty damn good," Roy said before acknowledging several lads that had just arrived at the pub.

"Wembley and this kind of stuff doesn't happen much for Millwall," Harry said. "The play-off semi-finals had me on the edge of my seat at the Den."

"It was touch and go with Scunthorpe United," Roy said as he watched a few lads carrying cases of Fosters 'amber nectar' Lager out of the front door.

"Tell me about," Harry said. "Five bloody bookings and it still ended goalless."

"That's just the way it goes sometimes," Roy said.

"Did you go to Scunthorpe's ground, Glanford Park, for the second leg?" Harry said.

"No mate," Roy said as he shrugged his shoulders.

"I'm skint, Harry, what I have on me today is all the money I have in the world," Roy thought. *"But with super Millwall at Wembley I just had to be here."*

"Shame, Roy, it was a good game," Harry said. "Scunthorpe took an early lead but Steve Morison levelled the game and then went on to set up Lee Gregory who smashed it into the back of the net just before half time. It was magic, pure magic."

"I didn't go to the match but I did what I always do with the Sun newspaper," Roy thought. *"I read every line and sometimes twice."*

"The Lions reigned victorious with a 3-2 finish and we're into the final!" Harry said.

The door of the pub slammed open and a young lad shouted out 'It's here!"

Roy and the rest of the Millwall lads filed through the pub door where they were met by an open top, bright red, vintage Routemaster bus parked outside.

"This is class," Roy thought as he looked at the open top bus. *"Absolute quality."*

Harry took a deep breath and belted out the start of Millwall's notorious chant and was quickly joined by all the lads.

"No one likes us
No one likes us
No one likes us

We don't care
We are Millwall
Super Millwall
We are Millwall
From the Den"

"This is going to be a brilliant day," Roy thought as the lads clambered on board the bus with case after case of Fosters Lager.

Roy climbed on board the Routemaster and took a seat upstairs. Within minutes tins of lager were being shared and passed around amongst the fans.

"Cheers," Roy said before cracking open the ice-cold tin of lager and taking a swig.

"Millwall at Wembley Stadium," Roy thought as he took a second sip of his beer. *"This is the kind of stuff dreams are made of."*

A couple of the lads hung St George's flags at the back and on both sides of the bus. Each flag had 'Millwall' written prominently in the middle and 'No One Likes Us'. The atmosphere on the bus was unlike anything else Roy had experienced at football.

"We're no longer the underdogs," Harry said as he held out his tin of lager for Roy to tap. "The highlight of the year, if not the decade, and here we are on our way to Wembley in an open top bus to see the Lions roar."

"Glorious," Roy said before taking a longer swig of his lager. "Truly glorious, and by all accounts there's going to be a good turnout numbers wise."

"There are thousands of us all over London and the home counties," Roy said. "It just takes a big game like this to bring them all together."

"This is our time," Roy thought as the bus trundled through the Saturday morning London traffic. *"All we have to do is stay focused on the prize and want it, really want that win."*

"There were 38,000 of us at Wembley in 2010," Harry said as he scrunched up the empty lager tin, placed it in the empty box, and reached for another.

"Yeah and we were victorious," Roy said triumphantly. "What a game!"

Harry took a long swig of his lager and leapt up onto his feet.

*"No one likes us
No one likes us
No one likes us
We don't care
We are Millwall
Super Millwall
We are Millwall
From the Den"*

Everyone had joined in. The raucous singing attracted the looks and curiosity from tourists, shoppers and the weekend workers. The bus crossed over into West London when a police car raced up behind the bus and put his siren on. Roy and several of the fans stood up and looked out the back of the bus.

"Old bill," Harry said.

"What do you expect?" another fan said.

"We ain't doing anyone any harm," Harry said. "They see Millwall and think immediately that we're worth a pull."

The uniformed police officers got out of their car and strolled up to the front of the bus.

"They want to make sure that we've got all the right licences and stuff to have alcohol on board," Harry said.

"Have we?" Roy said.

"I don't want to be spending time down the cop shop when I should be at Wembley," Roy thought.

"Yeah, of course we have," Harry said with a wry grin.

The lads watched as the driver handed the officers the documentation.

"What, no tooled up drug dealers who need locking up?" one lad called out.

"What's this then? You see Millwall and figure that it's got to be worth a tug?" another lad called out.

"More murders here in London now than New York City and you pull us over," Harry yelled out.

One of the officers studied the documents and then handed them back to the driver. Both officers turned abruptly and began walking back to the police car.

"YEAH!" Roy, Harry and the Millwall lads cried out together.

"No one likes us
No one likes us
No one likes us

We don't care
We are Millwall
Super Millwall
We are Millwall
From the Den"

The bus driver restarted the engine and slowly edged his way back out into the London traffic.

"They should be cracking down on the drug gangs, knife crimes and bloody terrorists," Harry hissed. "Not bothering with a bunch of excited Lions fans going to Wembley to witness the mighty Millwall seal their Championship promotion."

"Hoorah!" the lads called out before cracking open more tins of lager.

The Routemaster bus arrived in Wembley early and parked alongside coaches at a pub about fifteen minutes' walk from the Stadium. The pub was packed with Millwall supporters from all over the South of England.

"You should try and get to a few more away games next season," Harry said as he handed Roy a pint.

"Yeah, I will," Roy said as he looked down on the frothy head of the lager.

"If I had the money I'd go to every game, home and away and get a car and flat, and take Freya out to some special places," Roy thought as he sipped his lager. *"Instead I'm crashing at a mate's place, applying for jobs alongside hundreds of others while counting pennies and trying to make two and two equal five."*

Roy mingled with the fans while catching up with some old friends that he hadn't seen in years. The buzz inside the pub was euphoric with fans full of hope and desire for their team to do themselves and their loyal supporters proud.

"We are on the move," Harry called out.

Roy raised his glass and sipped thirstily at its contents before joining the hundreds of lads leaving the pub and marching, full of confidence, down to the stadium.

"There is nothing like Millwall away," Roy thought as he looked around at his mates. *"The solidarity between us is unbreakable. No fair-weather fans here, just hardcore lads who stick with their club through the good and the bad times."*

"This is it!" Harry said as he punched the air. "This is our team's biggest and most important day of the year."

"We will be triumphant," Roy thought as he approached the doors.

Following some initial hassle getting in, Roy and the lads made their way over to the middle tier in line with the penalty area.

"There's always some jobs-worth trying to spoil your day," one of the lads said before sitting down.

"He was lucky," Harry said, slowly shaking his head. "I can think of a dozen or so people that wouldn't have allowed him to finish his sentence. That twat would have been leaving here in an ambulance."

"Body bag more like it," another lad said.

As the Millwall players came out onto the field they were met with cheers and whistles.

"I've got to pinch myself," Roy thought as he watched Steve Morison and Lee Gregory warming up on the pitch. *"I can't believe we're here at Wembley."*

"Come on Morison!" Harry yelled, clapping his hands furiously.

At 3.00pm the mighty Millwall kicked off to a crowd of 53,000 cheering fans.

"Did you see that?" Roy cried out as Bradford City's Romain Vincelot fouled Lee Gregory just a few minutes into the game.

"He'll pay for that!" Harry said through gritted teeth.

The game continued at pace, with Bradford City conceding a corner from which Millwall's Shaun Hutchinson's powerful header sent the ball over Bradford City's crossbar. Millwall were under pressure but managed to defend their positions.

At half time the lads spoke avidly about the game and how they would have played differently or what individual players should have done to secure them an early lead.

There were no changes to either team as the second half began. Millwall defenders blocked a shot on the six-yard line and just minutes later, Lee Gregory's well-placed header gave Morison his shot but... it went wide. Millwall's defence came under pressure with two goal attempts before they made their first substitution with Shane Ferguson replacing Aiden O'Brien. The battle to win the championship continued with renewed vigour until Lee Gregory headed the ball across Bradford City's goal where Steve Morison volleyed the ball deep into the back of the net.

The Millwall fans leapt up onto their feet and cried out as they took the lead.

"That's the one," Roy said as he clenched both fists.

The singing Millwall fans drowned out all the other noises in the stadium.

"No one likes us
No one likes us
No one likes us
We don't care
We are Millwall
Super Millwall
We are Millwall
From the Den"

The match ran into five minutes of additional time. There was a scare from McMahon as his shot hit Millwall's side net, but the final whistle was blown and Millwall were the victors with a 1-0 win.

The fans were euphoric as they jumped up and down, punched the air and hugged each other. Roy grabbed hold of Harry as he cheered, and lifted him clean above his head as a handful of excited Millwall supporters ran onto the pitch.

"We had to defend our positions heavily," Harry said as Roy put him back on the ground. Harry continued to hop from his left to his right foot with excitement. "But Steve Morison did it. He brought back the bacon!"

"We stood strong as a team!" Roy said as he watched the crowds around him continue to celebrate the win.

"Bradford City played a good game," Harry said as he calmed down.

"Yes they did and you can't take that away from them," Roy said.

"Yeah but we won!" Roy thought as the buzzing sensation rose up from his stomach and flowed through his entire body.

"Right then, its back to celebrate at the Stanley Arms," Harry said as the lads began to make their way out of the stadium.

Within twenty minutes the lads, still singing from the tops of their voices, were back at the pub and clambering on board the open top vintage Routemaster bus.

There were still a couple of cases of Fosters lager on the bus which, despite being slightly warm, were passed around and gratefully received.

Roy cracked open his tin and took two huge sips.

"We are the champions!" Roy thought as the lukewarm lager slid down his throat.

The bus driver started the engine and drove slowly back towards South London with the Millwall fans singing at the tops of their voices all the way back to the Stanley Arms in Southwark.

The bus arrived back at the Stanley Arms with scores of lads raising their glasses and cheering.

"South London will be alive with Millwall supporters celebrating our Wembley win," Roy thought as he stepped down off the bus.

Before entering the pub, Roy took himself off to one side. He reached down into his pockets and brought out a few notes.

"I don't believe this," Roy thought as he shook off his frustration. *"I'm trying for job after job and getting nowhere fast and football,*

the one big love of my life, has my team winning at Wembley and here I am counting out a few quid to try and celebrate."

Harry and the lads ushered Roy into the pub. The atmosphere was euphoric with talk about travelling the country to away matches and what changes should be made. Roy nursed a couple of beers over several hours. Whilst in the toilet he checked what funds he had left and found just a few coins.

"Gutted, absolutely gutted," Roy muttered as he put his hand back into his pocket and shook his head vehemently.

Roy decided that rather than go back into the pub to say goodbye to his friends he would slip away through the back door and head back to Jenny's flat.

"If I say goodbye to one then you just know they'll be saying stuff like just have one more and I don't want to be explain that I'm skint, have no money and I'm pot-less," Roy thought as he stepped out of the back door into the road. *"It's embarrassing enough not having any money let alone having to explain it to your friends."*

Roy was feeling a little merry and the buzz of winning at Wembley hadn't quite subsided as he stood at the bus stop.

The bus arrived a few minutes later. Roy waved and got on.

"London Bridge mate," Roy said as he pulled out a few coins.

The bus driver looked down at the mix of small coins.

"Are you Millwall?"

Roy nodded.

The driver smiled.

216

"It was a good win today. Go on then," the bus driver said as he motioned Roy to take a seat.

"Cheers mate," Roy said as he turned and spotted a girl with locks of star flame golden hair that wreathed her moon shaped face.

Roy smiled and the girl smiled back.

The bus pulled away and Roy held tight onto each of the bars as he made his way to where the girl was sitting.

"Hi ya," Roy said with a broad smile.

"Hello, you look like you've had a good time," the girl said with a wry grin.

"It's been a brilliant day," Roy said as he sat back in the bus seat. "Are you from around here?"

The girl shook her head.

"Where do you live?" Roy said.

"Stepney," the girl replied

"Well I'm Roy, it's good to meet you."

"Likewise," said the girl.

"I'm Mandy."

"Mandy. That's a nice name," Roy said.

"Oh no that sounded lame, proper corny," Roy thought.

"Yeah. My mum and dad thought so too."

"Ouch. I should have seen that one coming," Roy thought.

"I'm not very good at this," Roy said as he sat upright. "You're a very pretty girl and I'm staying at a place near London Bridge. Would you like to come back for a coffee and maybe we could get to know each other better?"

"Jenny's away for a few days and I'm sure she wouldn't mind," Roy thought as he waited for Mandy's answer.

"I'm sorry but I have to be home and I'm already going to be late," Mandy said as she shrugged her shoulders.

"You are beautiful," Roy thought as he gazed into her eyes momentarily.

"Maybe we could meet another time," Roy said.

"Maybe," Mandy replied.

"Can I have your telephone number?" Roy said with a tipsy grin.

Mandy hesitated for a moment and then opened her handbag and took out a pen and a small piece of paper. She scribbled down her name and number and then handed it to Roy.

"Millwall," the bus driver called out.

Roy looked up.

"This is your stop."

Roy got up.

"I will call you, Mandy," Roy said before walking down the aisle and stopping briefly by the exit door to look back.

Mandy smiled and the automatic doors closed before the bus drove away.

"I could be right in there," Roy thought as he walked slowly through Borough Market towards Jenny's flat.

Chapter 19

May 23rd 2017

Roy had been up early and strolled down to the local newsagents where he bought his usual copy of the Sun Newspaper.

"I can't believe I lost that girl Mandy's number," Roy thought as the London traffic passed him by. *"She was beautiful and I think she liked me."*

Roy crossed the road.

"Gutted," Roy thought as he entered the shop.

Roy nodded at the owner and reached down for the Sun Newspaper. He paid and folded the newspaper in half before leaving the shop. Roy had a seat near the flats where he would sit to collect his thoughts and plan out his day. It was also where he would read his Sun Newspaper from front to back and then again during the evening.

The headlines read: Blast Rocks Manchester Arena above a photograph of a police officer helping a wounded woman.

"What the hell is happening to our country?" Roy thought as he read the article.

A suicide bomber had detonated a shrapnel laden bomb inside the busy Manchester Arena where American singer, Ariana Grande, had been performing earlier, as men, woman and children were leaving. Over twenty people had been killed and over one thousand injured, including young children.

Roy struggled to comprehend how a horrific attack like that could happen as he read the newspaper.

"Why are we allowing this to happen?" Roy thought as he raised his eyes from the print. *"Who is taking ownership of this undeclared war on the innocent citizens of this country and why are they not using all the resources available to remove the threat?"*

Roy read another couple of lines and then put the newspaper on the seat next to him.

"It doesn't seem that long ago that I was reading about the terrorist attack outside the Palace of Westminster," Roy thought as he stared up at the sky.

On March 22nd, 2017, Khalid Masood, a 52-year-old British citizen, drove a car erratically and mounted a pavement along the Westminster Bridge and Bridge Street. He injured over fifty people and killed four more before crashing his car into the palace perimeter fence. The stand-alone terrorist, wearing all black clothing, ran through to the corner of Parliament Square and through an open Carriage gate where he brutally murdered an unarmed police officer, PC Keith Palmer, with a knife before being shot dead at the scene.

"Surely those that govern us must have intelligence?" Roy thought. *"They must have a handle on all this."*

Roy found himself thinking about an article he read the previous year where Sadiq Khan, the Mayor of London, claimed that terror was all part and parcel of living in a big city.

"That's just an excuse by politicians for failing to protect the same people who gave them their job with a vote in the first place," Roy thought as he reached for his newspaper. *"This shouldn't be allowed to happen. Any person in government failing at their job should be fired and replaced by a more capable individual just as ordinary people are in the work place."*

Roy thumbed past the terror attack news and read the remainder of his paper before returning to Jenny's flat. He couldn't help thinking about the innocent children who had been injured while out on a special night to see their favourite singer, while images of the floor littered with blood stained nuts and bolts plagued his thoughts.

"I've got to get this stuff out of my head," Roy thought as he stared out of the window. *"I know, I'll pop in and check how Mum is doing. We can have a nice cup of tea and a chat about positive, upbeat, things."*

Roy had a pleasant few hours on the Ledbury Estate with his mum before stopping off at the Market Porter pub to have a drink with his friend Nelson.

"What are they?" Nelson said as Roy took a small packet of Champix pills from his jacket pocket.

Roy held up the packet.

"I take these to help with not smoking," Roy said. "Don't worry mate, I do get them on prescription."

"How is it going?"

"I'm getting there," Roy said. "What you have to do is be properly motivated to knock this smoking lark on the head, which I am."

222

"Okay," Nelson said before taking a sip from his drink.

"You just set yourself a date to stop," Roy said as he placed the packet on the table. "Then you can start taking these a couple of weeks before."

"You're not going to take them with lager, are you?"

"No of course not," Roy said with a chuckle. "You have to take these with water. I'm taking these twice a day and I was just checking to see how many I had left."

"So they work then?"

"I'll tell you in a couple of months," Roy said as he placed the pack back into his jacket pocket.

"Are there any side effects, mate?" Nelson said before motioning the bar tender to bring over another couple of pints.

"The doctor said it can make you feel a bit sick; you can have difficulty sleeping, or have crazy dreams," Roy said as the bartender placed a fresh pint in front of him.

"Cheers Nelson," Roy said as he reached for the glass.

"You're welcome mate," Nelson said as he raised his glass. "How are things with Tracy and Freya?"

Roy put his glass on the table before letting out a heavy sigh.

"Tracy and I gave life together a good go, but after fourteen years there was just so much stuff that happened and was happening that it just couldn't be fixed and I think we both knew that," Roy said.

"I'm sorry to hear that, mate," Nelson said. "What about your daughter, Freya?"

"I miss her and want to spend time with her mate, but I'm embarrassed and ashamed that my life is so full of shit right now," Roy said quietly. "I'm staying at a friend's place so I have no place of my own. I don't have a job, and believe me mate, it's not for the want of trying and I'm walking around skint most of the time. What kind of dad must I look like to her? So for right now I just keep my head down and try to crack on the best I can."

"I'm sorry to hear that, Roy," Nelson said warmly. "If I hear of anything on the work front you'll be the first to know."

"Cheers, Nelson I appreciate that," Roy said. "I do get to take the dogs out every day though."

"Oh yeah, I forgot you had dogs," Nelson said.

"Yeah we have a Husky called Copper and a Boxer dog called Toby," Roy said as his eyes lit up. "They're great dogs and I walk them most days along the Thames.

"That's good," Nelson said.

"Yeah, it gives me time to think and just enjoy being in the moment, if that makes sense," Roy said before reaching for his drink.

"I can imagine that walking those two dogs must be quite therapeutic," Nelson said.

"More than I'd care to admit," Roy thought.

***

Roy returned to Jenny's flat just before 10.00pm. He had only drunk a couple of pints courtesy of his friend, Nelson. Roy closed the bedroom door once he'd cleaned his teeth in the bathroom. He got undressed and climbed into bed. Roy turned on his side and closed his eyes. Images of him standing in front of a mirror holding out his empty pockets filled his mind. Roy turned over and curled into the foetal position and closed his eyes tighter.

Finally, after what had felt like hours, Roy felt an involuntary muscle spasm before drifting from a state of wakefulness to sleep:

"We are the Champions!" Harry yelled out from the top of his voice.

Roy had been transported back to the vintage Routemaster bus and returning to South London after the Lions win at Wembley.

Roy felt full of joy as he looked around at the jubilant friends he'd been supporting Millwall with since he was a teenager.

Hundreds of supporters lined the street cheering, waving flags and holding up their Millwall scarfs as the bus drove slowly past.

"That's the place," Harry said as he pointed to a pub with huge clear glass windows at the front that Roy couldn't recognise. "The drinks are on the house!"

Roy and the Wembley away day crew clambered off the bus and entered the pub while joyfully singing 'No One Likes Us'. Inside the bar, the line was a good ten metres long with over a dozen bar staff all wearing the official Millwall Polo shirts. Roy stood back and looked at the modern black granite custom built bar and the huge display of spirits.

"Come on Roy," Harry said as he slapped Roy on the shoulder. "Get a drink!"

Despite the scores of Millwall supporters, no fan was more than just one person away from being served at the bar.

"We're going the whole way now," Harry said as he raised his glass. "Can you imagine it, mate? Millwall in the Premier league?"

"I'll drink to that," Roy said, turning to his friends and raising his glass.

"Cheers!" they all called out as one.

Roy felt a strange shudder pass through his body followed by a freezing sensation that made him shake his hands. He turned to the door and saw several people, all dressed in black jeans and black T-shirts, file into the pub and form a line in front of the door.

"Something's not right here," Roy said as he turned to Harry.

"Have another drink," Harry said as he swallowed the last of his lager.

"I don't want another drink," Roy said as he looked at the motionless parade. "Something is definitely not right, I can feel it."

As one, the line of men pulled out huge machetes and raised their arms. One of the men stepped forward and yelled out something in a language that Roy didn't understand. The pub went quiet as all eyes turned to the men dressed in black.

"Arghhh!" the men all screamed out together before racing forward slashing the air wildly with their machetes.

"Run," Harry yelled, as he dropped his pint and fled towards the far wall.

The invaders screamed out as they cut, slashed and hacked their way into the celebrating fans who were trying to escape. The air with filled with intense fear, despair and great sadness as one fan after another was hacked, slashed and stabbed with blood stained knives

"This can't be happening!" Roy said as he watched one of the cruel, sadistic invaders thrust his knife deep into his friend Milton's chest. "Why are you doing this?"

Roy looked around at the carnage before him. The pub's floor was littered with the dead and injured bodies of his friends. Roy clenched his fists and gritted his teeth as he stepped over his dying friend Milton, and threw a mighty right hook, catching the attacker on the side of his face. Roy ducked as the machete passed over his head then bolted upright and threw a succession of rapid left and right hooks before launching a killer uppercut that sent the attacker sprawling over a pub table.

Roy looked up at the window to see blue flashing lights and a cacophony of police sirens.

The horrific carnage continued as his friends tried frantically to get away to safety but the invaders held the line and continued to kill, injure and maim all in their path.

"Come on, come on, help us!" Roy called out.

The flashing lights continued to flash and the police sirens had stopped but no one had come to their aid.

"My friends are dying in here!" Roy screamed.

Roy turned sharply to see an attacker racing towards him with a manic grin while slashing the air ferociously. As the killer raised and brought down his machete, Roy side stepped the attack and kicked the attacker's leg with all the strength he could muster. His leg buckled and he dropped the weapon. Roy grabbed his hair and looked down into the face of his attacker.

"What are you doing this?" Roy shrieked. "Why are you killing us? What have we done to you?"

"Death will come to you all!" the invader hissed.

Roy drew his fist back and delivered an almighty blow that broke teeth and shattered bones. The invader slumped to the floor. Roy looked back at the window and still the police were outside but no one was coming to help.

He was now facing four armed attackers.

Physical terror and panic struck him as they slowly walked towards him. He looked back at the window and could make out bodies moving back and forth in front of the flashing lights but still no one was coming.

"I will not run, I will not run," Roy muttered to himself over and over as the attackers continued to take small steps towards him.

Roy shook his hands, arms and shoulders and then bounced gently until he banished all fear. With both fists clenched he stormed into the killers while kicking, punching and jabbing fiercely as he fought for his right to live.

Suddenly Roy sat bolt upright in bed with both fists tightly clenched. He was dripping with sweat. A powerful, intense, futile feeling washed over his entire body.

"I've been dreaming," Roy thought as he struggled to move his legs from the bed to the floor.

Roy was physically and mentally exhausted.

Chapter 20

June 3rd 2017

Roy had walked Cooper, the Husky, and Toby, the Boxer along the Thames embankment that morning before settling down to read his Sun Newspaper. It was an unusually hot day with Roy having to remove his polo shirt.

"Right, what do we have here?" Roy thought as he scanned through the day's race fixtures.

Roy liked to have the occasional bet. It was always a small amount of money and motivated by a feeling he would have about a certain horse. He read through all the Doncaster fixtures but there was nothing that jumped out of the page. Roy ran his eyes down to the fixtures at Epsom Downs.

"Wings of Eagles," Roy thought as images of his friends Danny and Tony Eagle came to mind. *"That's it!"*

Roy placed the paper down by his side.

"I'll have a small each way bet," Roy thought as patted his pocket. *"I've got a good feeling about this."*

Shortly after Roy had placed his each way bet, his mobile phone rang and he saw that it was mate, Shaun Duhig.

Roy: Hello

Shaun: Hello mate, how are you?

Roy: Yeah, good Shaun. You know how it is.

Shaun: What are you doing later?

Roy: I've got nothing planned.

Shaun: Good, what about meeting me and a few mates at the Wheatsheaf in Southwark for the match.

Roy hesitated for moment.

Roy: Yeah, alright, but it'll just be for the match.

Shaun: Nice one, I'll see you there.

Roy: Take care mate.

The phone went dead.

"I hate this," Roy thought, shaking his head slowly. *"I hate counting pennies and being skint. All I want is a job and the opportunity to get my dignity back."*

The UEFA champion's league final was being played at the Millennium Stadium in Cardiff. Italy's Juventus were playing Spain's Real Madrid in a first ever European cup final held under a closed roof. The two teams had both previously fought their way to the finals in 1998 where Real Madrid took the trophy with a 4-1 win.

"It should be one hell of a game though," Roy thought as he put his hand in his pocket and felt the betting slip. *"Come on, Wings of Eagles, you can do it!"*

The day passed quickly with Roy taking the rare opportunity to soak up the British sunshine.

"Yes!" Roy yelled out as he punched the air.*" It's only gone and come in. Wings of Eagles has romped home!"*

Race five saw the horses at Epsom Downs off the line to a flying start at 4.30pm. Wings of Eagles and the jockey, P Beggy, ran furiously along the course and romped home, delivering Roy a £220 payday.

"I knew it," Roy thought as he gazed down at the twenty pound notes. *"Thank you Danny and Tony Eagle for the inspiration."*

Roy put £200 in the bedside cabinet and took out just £20. He checked his reflection in the mirror and then left Jenny's flat.

The Wheatsheaf pub was in Southwark Street Borough and just a stone's throw from London Bridge and in the heart of one of London's most popular food markets. It was favoured and admired for its craft, draft beers, pizzas and burgers.

Roy strode towards the pub while looking at the neon sign.

"I've got to make this twenty quid last," Roy thought as he entered the busy pub.

"This place is packed to the rafters," Roy thought as he spotted Shaun, Nelson and Old Mike. *"At least the lads have got a table with a decent view of the flat screen television."*

Roy raised his glass.

"It's good to see you Shaun, Nelson and Old Mike.

Everybody knew Mike as Old Mike because his son was also named Mike.

"Cheers," the lads said as they raised their glasses.

232

"It's packed in here," Shaun said as he glanced around the pub.

"What do you expect?" Old Mike said bluntly. "With two European Titans clashing at the Millennium Stadium?"

"Fair point," Shaun said as he winked at Roy.

"I didn't think Real Madrid would make it after being beaten by Atletico Madrid in the second leg of the Madrid Derby," Nelson said.

"That must have been one hell of a game," Roy said as he tugged at his Polo shirt collar.

"It's still bleeding hot," Roy thought. *"I don't think the sun bathing has helped much. I knew I should have used sun cream."*

"Who do you see as European champions?" Shaun said as he turned to face Old Mike.

"Real Madrid 2-1," Old Mike said as he reached for his ice cold lager.

"I'll have a fiver with you Mike that Juventus walk away with the European Cup," Shaun said confidently.

"Betting's a mugs game," Old Mike said with a shake of his head.

"Not for everyone," Roy thought as he patted his pocket.

"Alright let's make it for a pint," Shaun persisted.

Old Mike shrugged his shoulders.

"A pint it is then," Old Mike said as he held out his hand for Shaun to shake.

Shaun turned to Roy and Nelson.

"This is the eighth time in the Champion's League final for Juventus so I reckon they're hungry for a win," Shaun said as he sat back and pushed out his chest.

"Yeah, but they've only won twice, mate," Roy said with a chuckle.

"So you're with Real Madrid and Mike then?" Shaun said with a look of surprise.

"Whether you like it or not, Shaun, there isn't another club in Europe that can truly play the game when they have to," Roy said as he raised his glass and then decided to slow down. "It'll be Real Madrid."

"I'll have a tenner with you then," Shaun said as he reached into pocket and pulled out a wad of notes.

"I'd love to take your money, Shaun, but cash is tight and I have to make my little win last," Roy thought.

"No, you're alright," Roy said with a wink.

Roy turned to see that people were still entering the pub. He looked over at the bar, which was now three deep in thirsty customers, before continuing to nurse his own drink.

The match started with Juventus dominating possession for the first nineteen minutes of the game.

"You're going to owe me a pint," Shaun said as Juventus took their third major chance to score but failed.

"Early days," Old Mike said as he took a sip of his lager and winked at Roy.

Just one minute later Cristiano Ronaldo took possession and secured the first goal of the match.

"I told you," Old Mike said with a wry grin. "I can feel a feel a draft Guinness coming on."

"Yes!" Nelson yelled out as he punched the air.

"Now that was good football," Roy said.

"Granted," Shaun said, "But those Juventus boys will be back with a vengeance."

Mario Mandzukic of Juventus chested down a pass and hooked the ball over his shoulder. All four of the lads stood up as the ball rocketed into the back of the net.

"1-1"," Shaun said calmly.

"What a goal!" Roy said, looking down at the dregs in the bottom of his glass. "That will go down in history as one of the greats."

Nelson lifted his glass and then looked over at the bar.

"I don't think we're going to get a refill anytime soon," Nelson said before swallowing the last drops in his glass.

Juventus controlled the first half of the game while two Real Madrid players, Sergio Ramos and Dani Carvajal, were shown the yellow card.

Roy looked over at the bar which was four and five people deep.

"I fancy a proper drink," Roy thought.

"I'm going to pop back to Jenny's place to get some more money." Roy said as he stood up. "I'll only be about ten or fifteen minutes."

Once Roy was back at Jenny's place he washed, cleaned his teeth and changed out of his shorts and T-shirt. He reached into the wardrobe for his jeans and a freshly ironed Polo shirt before taking two twenty-pound notes from the bedside drawer. When he looked over at the clock, he realised that he'd taken longer than expected, so he strode back to the Wheatsheaf pub at pace.

The pub was still heaving and the second half of the championship match was already well underway. Roy stood in the doorway. The seats his friends were at were not taken and he couldn't see them anywhere.

"I bet they've gone back to Nelson's place, The Market Porter," Roy thought as he closed the pub door behind him.

Roy dialled Nelson's number on his mobile phone.

Nelson: Hello mate I was just about to call you.

Roy: Where are you?

Nelson: We couldn't get a drink, mate, so we're in the Market Porter.

Roy: I'm on my way.

Nelson: There will be a drink waiting for you on the bar, mate.

Roy scurried along the Borough Market to the Market Porter pub. There was no television for the game but they could talk, get a drink and didn't feel like sardines being crammed into a tin.

***

The Market Porter pub is one of the oldest and best Victorian pubs in all London and located in the heart of Borough Market.

"I love a pint in the Wheatsheaf," Nelson said as he handed Roy his drink. "But I can't bear queuing up."

"That makes two of us," Roy said.

Roy was pleased to see that 'Young Mike' was in the pub and sitting alongside his dad, 'Old Mike'. As they chatted about all things football, Katrina, the manager joined them.

Katrina was one of the managers and was bright and bubbly and an extremely attractive woman who made her customers feel instantly at ease. Roy couldn't help but notice how her swirls of long tawny brown hair toppled over her shoulders and veiled her pretty face.

"She's a lovely looking girl," Roy thought as Katrina smiled and sat down.

Word reached the pub that Real Madrid had won the championship game with an admirable 4-1 win.

Chapter 21

In Harold Hill, Khurum Butt, father of two and a Pakistani born British citizen was in the process of hiring a Renault Master van. He had tried to hire a 7.5 tonne truck but was refused on payment grounds.

Known by the police as a heavyweight member of the banned extremist group Al-Muhajiroun, he had a history of intimidating Muslims who had planned to vote in the 2015 elections, attempting to radicalise children and holding extreme views.

Khurum was joined by thirty-one-year-old Rachid Redouane, a pastry chef and failed asylum seeker whose application had been denied eight years earlier, and fast food worker Youssef Zaghba. With dual Moroccan and Italian citizenships, he travelled between the UK and Italy where the Italians monitored his every move having found, after a routine stop, ISIS related material on his mobile phone.

The hire van had been loaded with thirteen bottles of highly flammable liquid with rags stuffed into the necks of the bottles and blow torches.

Armed with 12-inch (30 cm) kitchen knives with ceramic blades which had been tied to their wrists with leather belts, the three Islamic extremists drove across London to London Bridge where they crossed at 21.58pm. Several minutes later they returned, with the driver keeping his foot flat on the floor as he rammed through the gears to build up speed. The Renault Van mounted the pavement three times and ploughed mercilessly into pedestrians.

The first 999 calls were made at 22.07.

The driver lost control and crashed through the central reservation. The tyres blew out and the Renault Master van crashed on Borough High Street.

Kharum, Rachid and Youssef clambered out of the van and ran down the steps to Green Dragon Court where they shouted out 'This is for Allah' before stabbing and killing five people outside a pub. The terrorists bounded back up the steps with the blood of innocents dripping from their blades. Police officers attempted to make an arrest but were stabbed, while angry members of the public jeered and threw bottles and chairs at the terrorists.

The three extremists ran around wildly, slashing and attacking people close to the bars and restaurants in Stony Street. A Romanian baker, Florin Morariu, battered one of the terrorists with a crate, before helping an injured police officer armed with a baton and leading twenty people to safety.

The three terrorists continued with their blood thirsty rampage through Borough Market to the Black & Blue Restaurant.

Chapter 22

Nelson was due to finish work at the Market Porter at 10.00pm and had agreed to meet Shaun, Old Mike and Young Mike at the Black & Blue Restaurant.

The Black & Blue Restaurant was a favourite for any and all occasions with their first class service, classic steaks and choices of wine. There was a large seating area by the bar and floor to ceiling glass panels the length of the restaurant.

The restaurant at the Black & Blue was busy, as always, with locals and tourists. Roy, Shaun, Old Mike and Young Mike ordered their drinks and sat at a table close to the main door.

"You owe me a pint," Old Mike said with a chuckle.

"Yeah, yeah, alright I'll get the next one in," Shaun said before turning to look out of the window.

"It looks busy out there," Shaun said as he watched people file past the window.

"It's the football," Roy said.

"Yeah of course," Shaun said before taking a sip from his pint.

The banter continued between the lads until Nelson arrived at the pub. Roy made sure that he had a drink waiting for him.

As the lads chatted, they couldn't help noticing the commotion upstairs. It was the sound of chairs scraping along the floor and falling over, along with fearful shouting and screams.

"I wonder what's going on up there?" Shaun said.

"Probably a fight," Old Mike said as he shrugged his shoulders.

"Nah, not in here," Roy said as he looked up at the staff milling around. "This is a trendy place and that kind of thing wouldn't happen here."

"What is going on?" Nelson said as he turned to see people jumping up out of their seats and looking out of the windows.

The lads heard a crash as a chair hit the dividing wall between the restaurant and the bar.

"It's all going off up there," Old Mike said.

All four of the lads turned to the glass wall as people outside in the market raced by. Moments later, after the last of the tourists bolted through the market, three men walked past the windows and peered in.

The manager bounded over to the door.

"What's he doing?" Roy thought as he watched him slam the glass door and lock it.

Khurum Butt, Rachid Redouane and Youssef Zaghba stood at the door with blood dripping from their knives.

"Run" Shaun said as he tapped Roy on the shoulder.

"Nah, we ain't done nothing," Roy said

The three terrorists, one wearing an Arsenal football top, began to kick furiously at the door while diners screamed and cried out. Others knocked over chairs and tables in their attempt to flee. The door held, but the kicking was ferocious and relentless, until finally the lower glazed panel began to give way. The stress, anxiety and emotion in the restaurant intensified as slowly, but very surely, the panel gave way, revealing a small entrance.

Roy sat firm.

10.13pm

One by one the terrorists crawled through the gap and stood in the doorway with their knives held by their sides.

"Allahu Akbar" one of the terrorists shouted before he slashed at the air, ran forward and sank his twelve-inch blade into Roy's chest. He withdrew it quickly and then stabbed Roy in the stomach.

Deep inside the amygdala the caveman survival instinct triggered a response faster than a single thought, allowing Roy's muscles to become more powerful, move and react faster to either fight the danger or take flight.

Roy jumped up with both fists tightly clenched and blood pouring from his chest and stomach.

"F**K you, I'm Millwall" Roy roared as he threw a left hook and followed it sharply with a powerful right piston punch that rocked the terrorist.

As the attacker's knees buckled, Roy struck him again forcing him down onto one knee. Roy looked up to see a second terrorist slashing wildly and racing towards him while screaming out "You killed our children!" The attacker sliced deep into Roy's head, neck and arm. Roy turned sharply and threw several punches, each one knocking the second attacker back. As the first attacker recovered and attempted to get back on his feet, Roy delivered a savage and devastating kick as though he were in a championship penalty shootout.

Roy could see Old Mike from the corner of his eye. He could see from the look on his face that his friend wanted to help him.

The third attacker had run towards the restaurant area yelling "Allahu Akbar"

The diners screamed and clambered over chairs, tables and each other in a bid to escape the flashing blade. In a state of panic and desperation some of the young men were scrambling over woman and children only to find themselves trapped at the back of the restaurant with no way of escape.

The third attacker looked back to see that one of his friends was down and Roy was wrestling with the second. He turned from the trapped diners and returned to the bar area where he slashed and stabbed at Roy.

"F**K you, I'm Millwall" Roy shrieked as he fought for his life.

While Roy single-handedly fought off the three armed terrorists with his bare hands, scores of men, women and children made their way down from the restaurant, behind the bar into the kitchen, and out to the safety of the street.

Roy could feel himself flagging. His arms felt heavy and weak.

"I must not go down!" Roy thought as mustered the strength to lunge forward and push over one of the attackers.

He turned and instinctively stumbled over to the small internal wall separating the bar from the restaurant. There were two diners huddled together and a couple of others hiding under the tables.

Roy staggered through the bar and into the kitchen before taking the exit into Borough Market.

10.14pm

"They wanted to kill me," Roy thought as he took pigeon steps away from the Black & Blue Restaurant.

He looked down at his blood soaked polo shirt.

"They stabbed me!" Roy thought. *"Where are my glasses?"*

Instinctively Roy staggered over to the Market Porter pub where he bashed on the door.

"Let me in, please, let me in," Roy pleaded and his knocks got weaker and weaker.

"I'm losing blood," Roy thought before turning on his heel and staggering away.

Roy could feel his legs give way. He dropped down onto one knee and reached for his mobile phone.

Roy: Jenny?

Jenny: Are you alright Roy?

Roy: I've been stabbed.

The phone went dead. He looked up and took a deep breath. The Market was like a ghost town.

"I must get to a hospital," Roy thought as he forced himself to stand back up and stagger down towards the High Street.

Roy battled to keep his eyes open and then his mobile phone rang.

Shaun: Roy, are you alright?

Roy: Shaun, mate, where are you?

Shaun: Me and a couple of others managed to barricade ourselves upstairs in the toilets. How are you?

Roy: I'm dying, they stabbed me.

Roy closed his eyes momentarily and dropped his phone. He continued to stagger down to the High Street to where an ambulance had come to a screeching halt.

"Thank you, thank you," Roy thought as he stumbled forward.

Roy knocked on the ambulance driver's window. The driver turned towards him.

"Help me, I've been stabbed," Roy said, trying desperately to stand upright.

The driver, with a look of sheer horror, rammed the ambulance shifter into gear, revved the engine and roared away.

"Where are you going," Roy thought as he watched the ambulance speed away. *"I'm dying."*

Roy took a couple of steps into the road when several police cars, with their blue lights flashing, came to an abrupt halt. The intense blue lights blinded Roy. He tried desperately to shield his eyes.

Roy raised his arm slowly and waved.

"Help me," Roy muttered

A marked BMW 4x4 armed response car rolled into view. Three fully equipped police officers from the Trojan Proactive Unit got out.

"Get down on the floor!" one of the officers ordered.

Roy dropped down to his knees and then fell clumsily forward onto the road. He raised his head slightly and through squinted eyes saw that the three knife wielding attackers were jogging towards him.

"They're coming to finish me off," Roy thought. *"This is it. I'm dead"*

10.16pm

BANG!

BANG!

BANG!

Roy watched as each one of the terrorists was shot dead.

"Come on son, let's get you out of here," a police officer said as he helped Roy to his feet and over to the safety of the police car.

The terrorists wore fake explosive belts, having strapped water bottles to their body with grey tape.

The Trojan officers continued to shoot at the explosive vests.

A second, friendly, officer carrying a first aid box attempted to bandage Roy's wounds.

"They stabbed me," Roy said.

The second officer stepped back and looked at the wounds in the light.

"These are too bad," the officer said before helping Roy into the police car. "We need to get you to the hospital."

As Roy lay across the back seat the car roared off at speed racing through the streets of London.

"Urgh" Roy called out as they bounced over a speed bump.

The police car sped over a second speed bump.

"Can you slow down? These bumps are making me hit my chin."

The police officer maintained the speed and radioed ahead to St Thomas Hospital.

Roy could feel a flushing sensation in his chest. He wanted to close his eyes, he was tired, but the bumps forced him to stay awake.

"Stop touching your ear," The police officer in the passenger seat said as he turned to check on Roy. "It's hanging off!"

Chapter 23

T he tyres on the police car squealed as it came to a sudden stop.

"I think I might be dying," Roy thought as the nurses opened the rear door and helped him out of the car and onto a trolley bed.

"What is your name?" a nurse asked as she cut away Roy's blood-soaked clothing.

"Roy, Roy Larner,"

Roy closed his eyes as his clothing was removed.

"You're in good hands now, Roy," the nurse said with a warm smile.

As an image of Freya entered his mind his eyes shot wide open.

"Please tell my daughter, Freya, where I am," Roy pleaded. "I can't die without seeing my daughter."

As the morphine took effect Roy felt like he was riding a rollercoaster with images of his daughter, Freya, flashing before him first as a baby, then as a toddler, and then images of her in her first school uniform pulsated back and forth.

"What is happening to me?" Roy thought before slipping into unconsciousness.

"Roy, Roy, what is your address?"

Roy opened his eyes slowly. He struggled to open his mouth and the few words he could muster were slurred and jumbled.

"After three," the lead nurse said to her team before counting down and lifting Roy onto an MRI scanning tube.

The MRI, magnetic resonance imaging, is a type of scan that uses strong magnetic fields and radio waves to produce detailed images of the inside of a body.

The team of nurses patched up all of Roy's major stab wounds and stitched the lacerations on his head and neck, before sewing his ear back on. He was taken to a room where he finally fell into a deep, dreamless, sleep.

***

Roy opened his eyes.

"Where am I?" Roy thought as he slowly looked around the room. *"There's an armed police officer at the door. Why is there an armed police officer here?"*

The memory of the night before slowly came back to him.

"My arms, I can't move them!" Roy thought as he tried desperately to move them.

Roy began to panic. His breathing became rapid and he was short of breath. His heart thumped violently against his chest and he began to sweat.

"I've lost the use of my arms!" Roy thought.

The armed officer turned to Roy and nodded.

Roy returned the nod before closing his eyes.

"I'm confused," Roy thought. *"What has happened to me?"*

"Good morning Mr Larner."

Roy opened his eyes to find a doctor standing over his bed with a clip board.

"What has happened to me?" Roy said. "I can't move my arms."

"You've suffered lacerations to your arms, Mr Larner," the doctor said, placing the clipboard back at the bottom of the bed. "You have injured the nerves. This kind of injury can cause numbness and a loss of feeling."

Roy remained quiet as he tried to process what he was being told.

"We're taking you now to the plastic surgery team," the doctor said as the ward orderly released the bed brakes and began to wheel Roy out of the room.

Roy fell in and out of a deep sleep over the next two days. His memory of the conversations that took place were vague. The only constant was the warm smile from the nurse every time she checked in on him. The armed officer remained vigilant at the door.

"How do you feel today?" the nurse asked before taking his temperature.

"Okay," Roy mumbled.

"You're stable and no longer on the critical list," the nurse said as she made notes on the pad. "You're not allowed to have visitors but one of your friends, Shaun, has been incredibly persistent."

"Shaun is a good friend," Roy said as he gently moved his arm.

"They're working again!" Roy thought as a wave of relief swept over him.

"Nurse," Roy said.

"Could you please ask Shaun, when he next comes in, to get me a mobile phone?" Roy said.

"I can do that for you," the nurse said before racing off to see her next patient.

Later that evening the nurse returned with a black Nokia phone. Roy thanked her before calling Shaun.

Roy: Shaun, is that you mate?

Shaun: Mate, you have no idea how good it is to hear your voice.

Roy: I thought it was all over.

Shaun: After what you went through Roy, we all thought you were in big trouble. Anyway, I'll give you an update. I've been around to Tracy's place and put her in the picture. She wanted to visit before going on holiday to Turkey but I told her she couldn't at the moment.

Roy: What about Freya?

Shaun: She wasn't there mate, and I thought that kind of news comes best from her mum.

Roy: Yeah, right.

Shaun: I've called all your brothers, Roy, and seen your mum.

Roy: Thank you mate.

Shaun: No thanks needed. It's what mates do. Roy, social media has just gone mad.

Roy: Why, what have I done?

Shaun: People are calling you a hero mate

Roy: What?

Shaun: They're calling you the Lion of London Bridge

Roy: Are you winding me up?

Shaun: No mate, straight up. I'm not kidding when I say that most of the UK wants to buy you a pint.

Roy: I don't know what to say.

Shaun: I've been reading through some the comments:

- ❖ *Super cool nickname and he earned it!*
- ❖ *Big brass British balls coming back in style*
- ❖ *I hope the legend recovers and lives a very long rewarding life*
- ❖ *Best wishes for a speedy recovery Mr Larner*
- ❖ *All the best Mr Larner you made me feel proud to be British again.*
- ❖ *What Roy did was ballsy and selfless. I can only pray that I'd measure up to his example in the same circumstances.*

Roy: That will do mate. I don't know what to say.

Shaun: There are a lot more, Roy.

Roy: I'll find out when you can visit and let you know.

Shaun: I'll be there.

Roy hung up just as the nurse was coming back to check on him.

"Nurse, when can I have visitors?"

"I'll check for you, Roy, but I expect once we've moved you tomorrow you'll be okay to see family only.

"I wanted to see Shaun," Roy thought. *"Knowing Shaun he'll find a way to get in."*

"Thank you," Roy said.

"I've never known so much press and media attention before," the nurse said with a sigh.

"What do you mean?" Roy said.

"There have been newspaper reporters, photographers and television film crews from all over the world wanting to interview you," the nurse said as she tucked the corners of his bed linen in. "The hospital security are working overtime to keep them at bay."

"Why?" Roy said as he shrugged his shoulders. "I really don't understand all this."

"What you did Roy, was truly heroic and embodies the best values of western culture," the nurse said. "Now try and get some rest."

Roy rested his head back on the pillow and waited for the nurse to leave before reaching for his mobile phone and dialling Tracy's mobile number.

"I just want to check in with Freya and let her know that her dad is okay," Roy thought as he held the phone to his ear.

There was no answer.

"Of course, Tracy is in Turkey. I hope Freya's not worrying about me" Roy thought as he cancelled the call. *"Where are my glasses?"*

Roy had lost his glasses at Borough Green.

"Mr Roy Larner?"

Roy looked up to see two men showing their warrant cards to the armed guard.

The police officers explained that they needed to take a written statement so that they can collect evidence and understand exactly what happened.

"We understand that this is a difficult time Mr Larner," the police officer said as he pulled a seat up next to the bed. "It is important that we collate the facts while they're still fresh in your mind. You can, of course, take a break at any time. Would you like somebody to sit here with you or a legal representative?"

"A solicitor?" Roy said as he struggled to sit upright. "Why would I need a solicitor? I haven't done anything wrong."

"I understand that," the officer said as he sat back in his chair. "I'm just advising you of your rights."

"My rights? What is this?" Roy thought as he stared at the officer. *"Am I under arrest?"*

"On a personal note, Roy," the second police officer said with a genuine smile. "What you did was incredibly brave. There are a great many people out there who believe that they would do what you did, but very few would actually do it. I, for one, take my hat off to you."

Roy gave his statement to the best of his ability. The police returned to the hospital three times during his stay.

As Roy rested his head on the pillow he received a text message saying that a friend and fellow Millwall supporter, Jayne Jacobs, had set up a GoFundMe page for him to replace his lost glasses.

GoFundMe is an American crowdfunding platform that allows people to raise money for events, celebrations and challenging circumstances.

Terry Argyle, a QPR supporter and good friend, told the hospital receptionist that he was one of Roy's brothers and managed to get in to see him.

Chapter 24

Tuesday 6th June

Roy could hear a broad Geordie accent at the hospital door.

"Is that you Roy?" a huge Geordie fella said as he stepped into Roy's room.

Roy nodded.

"Look, I hope that you don't mind the intrusion, I'm Tony Davis, and after hearing what you did at London Bridge I just had to stop by.

"Tony Davis?" Roy said.

"That's right."

"Tony Davis the Olympic boxing trainer?" Roy said.

Tony nodded.

"I read about you," Roy said as he motioned Tony to sit down. "You were on Westminster Bridge when a terrorist killed five people and then stabbed a police officer.

Tony nodded.

"Yeah, that would have been PC Palmer."

"You tried to save him," Roy said, trying to sit upright.

"I was at a nearby community event with the British Lionhearts amateur boxing team when it happened," Tony said. "I just did what anybody would have done."

The two men talked about what had happened at London Bridge and Roy's injuries.

Tony Davis, an ex-serviceman, was the first to run to the aid of PC Keith Palmer, the unarmed police officer, who was stabbed as he attempted to stop terrorist, Khalid Masood, outside the Palace of Westminster. Tony attempted to revive PC Palmer with CPR. Unfortunately PC Palmer died at the scene. Kalid Masood continued to cause havoc before being shot dead by an armed officer.

"You will need to speak to somebody about all this at some point," Tony said. "Make sure that you get the right help."

"I'm fine and thank you for stopping by. It's been an honour meeting you," Roy said with a painful grin.

"The honour has been mine," Tony said as he waved goodbye.

What a genuine, lovely, fella," Roy thought as he took a shot from his inhaler and relaxed his head back into his pillow. *"He took time out to visit me, Roy Larner, from the Ledbury Estate, Peckham."*

***

Roy had agreed to an interview with Matt Wilkinson from the Sun Newspaper the following day. His friend, Shaun, had told the nurses earlier that morning, that he was Roy's brother and had brought him a Millwall flag which he placed by the right side of his bed.

Roy told the journalist that he had been a Sun reader since his school days. When told that the 'GoFundMe' page had raised over thirty thousand pounds to aid his recovery from people who had been inspired by his heroism, he was shocked and humbled by such generosity.

Roy posed with the Millwall flag for the photographer before turning his head so they could photograph the horrific injuries to his ear and neck. Roy posed with the book 'Learn to Run', an amusing gift from his friend Aiden Andrews.

The interview went well and the Sun newspaper's feature generated sacks full of 'Get Well Soon' cards and messages from members of the public all over the United Kingdom, America and Europe. When left on his own he opened and read each and every message.

Charles Bronson, dubbed by the British Press as 'Britain's Most Notorious Prisoner' very kindly sent Roy a hand drawn picture entitled 'Legend Roy'. The management of Xhamster sent him six bottles of beer and a box of two hundred condoms while another company, Frequency Beer Works wanted to produce a brand of beer named 'Fxxk You I'm Millwall'.

Saturday 10th June

Roy had been moved to another more comfortable, private room on the top floor. It had a television and the solitude gave Roy the time his body needed to rest and physically recover. However, with help, he managed to go downstairs to meet with his friends from Millwall. He passed an elderly lady in the corridor. Her face lit up when she saw him and she immediately threw her arms around his bandaged body. She hugged and squeezed Roy while whimpering 'thank you so much for what you did'. After wiping the tears from her eyes, she leaned forward and kissed Roy on the cheek.

Roy thanked her and wished her well.

The Lions cheered loudly as The Lion of London Bridge came into view. A sudden rush of excitement flowed through Roy's body as he looked around at the twenty plus friendly, familiar, faces. Memories of football, lad's days out and socialising at the pub filled his mind as his Millwall mates patted his back and teased him with traditional laddish banter.

"These are my friends, my good friends and I'll remember this day for the rest of my life," Roy thought as he raised his heavily bandaged hands and arms.

Tuesday 6th June

Roy had gained permission to leave the hospital to attend an interview on 'Good Morning Britain' at their London studios at 6.00am. Roy explained to the producers that he had literally nothing to wear as his blood soaked clothes had been cut off when he first arrived. The studios, very kindly, arranged for a white t-shirt, trousers and trainers to be sent to the hospital for him to wear. The taxi arrived in good time and once the nurse had double checked his bandaging, he was driven through London to the studios where the team welcomed him. The weather presenter, Laura Tobin, shook Roy's hand warmly. She chatted continuously which helped Roy to calm his nerves until he was sat on the sofa alongside Piers Morgan and Susanna Reid.

Roy's heart was racing as the cameras turned towards him. He struggled to hide the confusion and trauma that persisted in plaguing his mind.

Journalist, writer and television presenter Piers Morgan introduced Roy as a special guy just out for a drink when the London Bridge Terror attack kicked off. He explained that everyone was running for cover but Millwall fan, Roy Larner, fought off three armed jihadis in an act of extraordinary heroism. Roy tried to describe the events while struggling with the enormity of what had happened and now appearing on national television.

The Good Morning Team had all been extremely friendly and helpful. Piers Morgan had been a genuine nice guy. Directly after the interview Roy returned to the hospital where he had surgery to repair his diaphragm.

Debra Alessi, the founder of the 'Face Forward' charity in Los Angeles California reached out to Roy while he was in hospital.

Face Forward is a non-profit organisation which Debra Alessi began in 2007. They provide pro-bono physical and emotional reconstruction for battered men, women and children who have been victims of domestic or gang violence. Their mission is to help the victims recover from their physical and emotional scars so they may be able to regain their self-confidence, and lead a productive life when re-entering society.

Debra invited Roy to an event they were hosting in Los Angeles to receive an award. He would be joined by Mel B and Ozzy Osborne. She went on to explain that her husband had a plastic surgery practice and that he would help Roy with the scars he had. The conversation closed with Debra saying that she would send the air tickets and that he would be collected from the airport. Roy felt honoured and touched by the kind gesture. It brightened his day.

Unfortunately Roy could not get a visa soon enough to attend the event. Debra did, however, maintain contact with Roy and asked for regular updates on his physical and mental health.

Freya visited on the Sunday with both dogs. The security guard had been extremely helpful in helping Roy to maintain balance and stayed with him throughout the visit. Seeing Freya and the dogs wagging their tails was an incredibly emotional moment.

"I could have been killed and never seen my beautiful daughter and those damn dogs ever again," Roy thought as he held back tears.

Costas visited in the afternoon. He wanted to talk but Roy had struggled to stay focused as he was desperately tired. Costas stayed for one hour.

***

The time came for Roy to leave the hospital. He made a point of thanking every nurse who had helped with his recovery.

"You're very brave, son," the uniformed police officer said as he Roy passed him in the corridor. "You're probably on the ISIS hit list now."

"What?" Roy thought as he watched the officer shake his head. *"I'm on a hit list now?"*

Tracy arrived and helped Roy to pack up his few belongings along with the sacks of 'Get Well' cards. The staff very kindly helped to bring them all down to the front of the hospital and waved a black London cabbie over.

"Hello matie," the cab driver said as he helped place Roy's belongings in the back of the cab.

"Hello mate," Roy replied.

Roy had always admired the black cab drivers of London believing that earning the credentials, 'The Knowledge' to drive that iconic taxi must have been the equivalent of earning a university degree. Any passenger, anywhere, could get into the black taxi and give an address and instantly the cabbie has to know the most direct route.

Roy and Tracy got into the back of the taxi.

"How are you feeling?" Tracy asked as the taxi pulled away.

Roy waved to the hospital staff that had been so good to him during his stay.

"I'm fine," Roy said as he turned and sat back in his seat.

"Are you sure you want to do this?" Tracy said.

The president of the World Boxing Council (WBC), Jose Sulaiman, had reached out and extended an invitation to Roy to attend a black-tie dinner function at the Mayfair Sporting Club. It is one of four major organisations which sanction professional boxing bouts.

"It's an honour," Roy replied.

"I know that, Roy, but should you really be doing this on the same day that you're leaving hospital?" Tracy said, tilting her head.

"I've said that I will," Roy said.

The taxi driver drove towards London Bridge when Roy spotted Freya standing with several of her friends.

"Cabbie, can you stop please?" Roy said.

The taxi driver checked his rear-view mirror before coming to a stop.

Tracy opened the cab door.

"Freya," Tracy called out.

Freya looked over at the black London taxi cab and her eyes lit up when she saw that Roy was sitting on the back seat. She quickly said her goodbyes to her friends and raced over to the taxi cab.

"Dad!" Freya said as she clambered into the back of the cab.

"I love you Freya," Roy thought as he watched his daughter sit beside her mum.

The taxi dropped them back at Tracy's home where Roy managed to get showered and changed.

"I know this is probably too soon," Roy thought as he attempted to dry himself. *"But I've said that I will and I never go back on my word."*

Roy stepped into a leg of his trousers and gently tugged them up before placing his leg into the second leg.

"The hospital staff were amazing," Roy thought as he buttoned his trousers. *"They even brought me up a full English breakfast with eggs, bacon and sausages at the end of my first week."*

Tracy helped Roy get his jacket on and watched as he walked gingerly out to the waiting taxi cab.

Roy enjoyed the evening at the Mayfair Sporting Club, but did find the whole experience a little overwhelming. There were lots of smiling faces, back slapping and congratulations before Roy posed with the award the WBC had very kindly given him in recognition of his outstanding bravery.

Later, when Roy returned home, he found himself thinking about the police officer's comment.

"Have ISIS really added me to some kind of hit list?" Roy thought and he edged himself onto the bed. *"All this has happened so fast. I'm not sure that I've truly come to terms with all this yet."*

Roy stared up at the ceiling while allowing his eyes to adjust to the dark.

"Maybe ISIS doesn't even have a hit list and the officer was just surmising?" Roy thought *"I've not read anything about hit lists."*

Roy wanted to turn over and lay on his side but he knew that his injuries would make it too painful.

"I need to talk to someone, just in case." Roy thought as his heart pounded against his chest. *"What kind of action must I take to safeguard my family and close friends?"*

Roy could feel himself break out into a mild sweat.

"There is nothing to fear but fear itself," Roy thought as he took several shots from his inhaler in a bid to control his breathing and bring down his heart rate. *"I'm sure it was Franklin D Roosevelt who said that."*

Roy finally fell into a deep, dreamless, sleep a little after 2.00am.

Chapter 25

"*This place is the absolute pits,*" Roy thought as he looked around the single bedsit room.

Roy had been told to move into a single room two sets of stairs above a barber shop in Brixton. The room had torn wall paper from the 60s, a single bed and had a strong, almost overpowering, musty smell of damp.

Roy slumped back on the bed and exhaled loudly.

"*Why do I feel so damn low, empty and completely hopeless,*" Roy thought as he looked at his heavily bandaged hands and arms before looking up at the brown stained ceiling. "*I feel constantly on edge and I'm looking out the window for those terrorists. Are they coming for me like the police officer said?*"

Roy reached for his inhaler.

"*I can't sleep because I have to be ready for when they come back for me and if I do sleep then the nightmares are too vivid and beyond horrific,*" Roy thought as he placed his inhaler back into his pocket. "*I've been stuck in here for weeks. Is this it now, is this my life?*"

Roy gritted his teeth. He wanted to raise his right hand, clench it into a fist and pound it down on the bed with tremendous force.

"*I'm angry, irritated and frustrated and I need help, proper help,*" Roy thought as he shook his head slowly. "*I'm hungry but can't be bothered to go out and eat. Who am I kidding? I'm climbing up the* walls with anxiety. Was all this my fault? Am I, somehow, to blame for all of this?"

Roy closed his eyes.

"Why can't I just have one decent night's sleep without being stabbed over and over," Roy thought as he closed his eyes tighter. "I miss my daughter, my mum, my friends and my life!"

"Maybe I shouldn't have fought back so hard and just let those Jihadis kill me or even run when I had the chance," Roy thought as he rubbed his chin. "Everybody else ran, including police officers, so why did I just front up three tooled up lunatics intent on killing everyone with nothing but harsh language and my fists?"

Roy slammed his fist down on the bed for a second time.

"I feel so damn tired but I don't want to sleep," Roy thought as sat up and then walked over to the window.

"I can't keep doing this day after day and night after night," Roy thought as he peered down from behind the curtains onto the busy street.

Another long night slowly passed into day. The light from the lamppost shone through the window and lit up part of the room.

"I need to get out of here, but I'm not safe in London," Roy thought as he sat bolt upright on the bed. "Maybe if I move far away then all this will pass."

Roy allowed himself a small, brief, smile.

"That's it," Roy thought as a surge of hope raced through his body. *"I'll move as far away as possible until all this blows over. I'll make a start first thing in the morning!"*

It was after 4.00am before Roy finally fell into a restless sleep where he, once again, relived the London Bridge attack. His body jerked wildly as the image of the terrorist thrusting the ceramic blade into his chest and then his stomach plagued his dreams.

Chapter 26

Roy gathered up the courage to travel down to New Romney in Kent where he bought a static caravan.

"I hate having to leave London, my life and everyone and everything behind, but what choice do I have?" Roy thought as he looked at his new home.

New Romney is a market town and popular holiday destination close to the Kent coast. Roy's spacious static caravan was housed on a complex which included a grocery shop and a large club house where holiday makers could come to shake off the stress of work, enjoy a few drinks and be entertained by the activities.

A couple of the workers recognised Roy from the tabloids and television. They smiled and simply waved which suited Roy. He was desperate not to bring any attention to himself. Roy was never one to drink at home as he preferred company and a pub atmosphere. Whilst there were times when he craved company, he chose, for safety's sake, having visited the club house just twice, not to make it a regular thing. Instead Roy would leave his new home at sunrise and walk for miles along the beach. Some days he would turn right and walk along the beach to Lydd, the most southerly town in Kent and on others he would turn left and stroll up to Dymchurch and on to Sandgate.

Roy had dumped his Android phone to avoid social media contact and bought himself a very simple, pay as you go, Nokia mobile phone.

At first the relief of being away from London had eased his anxiety slightly, and he was rewarded with the occasional nightmare free sleep but the solitude slowly but very surely seeped into his subconscious and reawakened the fear of being recognised.

Within a few short weeks Roy would jump up from his seat at the slightest noise outside and peep through the curtains and then get angry with himself when it turned out to be a neighbour simply coming or going.

Roy had a phone call from David Allport who represented the government's 'Prevent Programme'. He informed him that he would be visiting and gave Roy a date and time to expect him.

"What I would give just to have a normal night out with a few mates," Roy thought as he stared aimlessly out of the caravan window. *"Just good old football chat and a few drinks with like-minded people instead of being stuck here at the far end of Kent and a million miles away from civilisation as I know it."*

Roy ventured around to the grocery store for milk, tea bags and coffee and whilst he would have enjoyed a drink, he didn't pick up any alcohol.

"Drinking alone just isn't the same," Roy thought as he quickly scanned over the bottles of Hardy's red and white wines. *"An ice-cold pint of lager with my mates and a night of good laughs is what's really needed right now because the occasional trip for a hospital appointment just isn't doing it."*

Once back in the caravan Roy took a shot from his inhaler before putting the kettle on.

"I'll have a nice cup of tea and read The Sun," Roy thought as put the teabag into the mug. *"Who knows, maybe there will be something in the horse racing section that just jumps out at me. A small flutter might break the day up."*

As Roy say down on the settee and placed the steaming hot mug of tea on the side table his mobile phone rang.

"Who can that be?" Roy thought as he reached for the phone.

Roy: Hello, who is this?

Caller: Roy, mate, how the hell are you? It's Eric.

Roy: Eric! Good to hear your voice mate. Yeah, I'm alright, you know, getting by.

Eric: You need to get yourself back here.

Roy: I can't just at the moment.

Eric: Millwall Football Club have come out and said they're proud to have you as a supporter and want you to come to the Den when they play Bolton on the 12th.

Roy: Really?

Eric: Damn right mate. You're a legend mate, and you shouldn't forget it.

"It doesn't feel like that mate," Roy thought as he listened to Eric tell him about the arrangements.

Eric: So what can I tell them, will you be there?

"I want to go, I want go!" Roy thought as he tried desperately to suppress the anxiety growing in the pit of his stomach.

Roy: It's Millwall, I'll be there!

Eric: Brilliant, get yourself booted and suited mate because you'll be pressing palms with the best.

Roy: I will mate.

Eric: I don't know if you know this mate, but there have been people from all over the country calling for you to be awarded the George Cross.

Roy: What, really?

Eric: I'm not kidding. I doubt if it'll have legs, but for what you did, mate, you deserve it. There are people out there who would have been seriously stabbed up if it wasn't for you, and that should be recognised.

Roy: I don't know. I'm just a working-class guy from South London, so I doubt if I fit the profile of a man worthy of that kind of medal.

Eric: What you did is exactly the kind of thing that deserves a medal and don't you forget it!

"A George Cross, for me, Roy Larner," Roy thought as he held the phone to his ear. *"I'd feel like the proudest man on the planet, but it'll never happen."*

Roy: It's been great hearing your voice, Eric, please let everyone know that I'll be there.

Eric: Will do mate. There will be stands full of lads pleased to see you back on the manor.

Roy: Take care mate.

Eric: You too.

Roy hung up.

"Millwall Football Club management want me at the Den," Roy thought as a smile spread across his face. *"What an honour."*

Roy picked up the newspaper and read the headlines and then placed it on the settee next to him.

"What if ISIS are waiting for me?" Roy thought

Roy took a sip of his tea.

"With over eight thousand hard-core Millwall supporters, ISIS would need an army because we don't run, period," Roy thought as he took a second small sip. *"I'm going and that is that!"*

Until the day of the Millwall v Bolton match, the nightmares and paranoia intensified but nothing, no matter how brutal the visions in his head played out, would stop him from going to the Den.

Roy had dressed himself in a smart blue suit and had polished his shoes so he could see his face in the reflection. He battled with the intense, excessive, worry that ISIS would be waiting for him back in London.

The New Romney taxi took Roy the fourteen miles to Folkestone Station where he travelled back to London and on to meet mates before going to the Den.

"This feels like home," Roy thought as he approached the ground. *"I have missed this place so much."*

The home and away supporters filled the stands and Roy could hear and feel the supporter's excitement for the game to come.

Roy took two long shots from his inhaler.

"That could have been my life out there playing professional football," Roy thought as he looked down at his inhaler. *"Who knows, maybe I could have even played for my country. What an absolute honour that would have been."*

The press and management signalled Roy and the other VIP guests that it was time.

Roy took a deep breath and strutted out onto the pitch with Grant Merrill, Kenny Gerard, and Danny Kenny. Millwall supporters, the visiting Bolton fans, groundsmen, club management and security immediately rose to their feet and began to clap their hands furiously, showing respect and cheering loudly. The raucous clapping continued with Millwall breaking into their infamous chant:

"No one likes us
No one likes us
No one likes us
We don't care
We are Millwall
Super Millwall
We are Millwall from the Den!"

The crowds continued to chant and cheer as management placed medals around the lads' necks while photographers snapped furiously.

"I'm home," Roy thought as he looked out at the sea of cheering Millwall supporters.

The game concluded with a 1-1 draw.

***

The trek back to New Romney after the game was long and lonely. When several Asian lads boarded the train Roy clenched his fists tightly.

"They've been following me," Roy thought as he watched the lads sit down and engage in what appeared to be light hearted chat. *"They were waiting for me to be on my own."*

Roy looked around the carriage and considered moving.

"But they look like everyday blokes," Roy thought as he watched the lads laugh amongst themselves. *"Maybe they're not ISIS fighters out looking for me."*

Roy weighed each of the lads up in his mind while playing out a spectacular fight scenario which would leave him victorious until the anxiety kicked in.

"What if they're all tooled up with knives or guns?" Roy thought. *"I'll be done in, stabbed up and left to die in a pool of blood and guts on a bloody train into Kent"*

At the next station the lads all left the train.

Chapter 27

Roy looked up and clenched his fists when he heard a knock at the caravan door.

"Who is it?" Roy called out as he stood with feet apart and both fists tightly clenched. ready for whatever was to come at him from behind the locked door.

"I'm ready, I'm ready," Roy thought as the adrenaline raced around his body.

"Hello Roy, its Dave Allport from Rewind UK regarding the Prevent Programme. I think you're expecting me."

Roy relaxed his stance, took a deep breath and then reached over and opened the door.

Dave had a medium build, short dark hair and Roy estimated him to be in his mid to late thirties.

"Come in," Roy said as his heartbeat began to slow down.

Dave entered the caravan and Roy motioned him to sit on the sofa.

"That's not a London accent," Roy said.

Dave shook his head.

"No, I'm a Brummie, you know, from Birmingham," Dave said as he sat down.

"Oh, right," Roy said as he filled the kettle with water. "I'm going to make a coffee, would you like one?"

"No, I'm fine but thank you," Dave said as he relaxed into the seat.

"How are you, Roy?" Dave said with a half grin.

"You mean after having fought off three armed terrorists, getting stabbed eight times and multiple lacerations only to be told by the police that I'm probably on the ISIS hit list now?" Roy said sarcastically.

"Yes, I've been reading your file on the way here, Roy, you've certainly gone through a lot," Dave said.

"Did they tell you that they moved me to this slum in Brixton with just a bed and nothing else and told me that I couldn't go out?" Roy said as he spooned a heap of coffee into a mug.

Dave nodded.

"They also mentioned that you upset the local MP," Dave said as he shook his head slowly.

Roy could feel himself tense up but then closed his eyes and took a deep breath before pouring the hot water in the mug.

"I needed help! I still need help!" Roy said as he stirred the hot drink. "I asked him nicely but he wasn't listening, and I felt like I was just being brushed off as if I didn't matter, that what I did didn't matter, and I was just a hindrance."

"Yes, I have read that report," Dave said.

"It got heated and I said some things that I regret but calling the police on me and having me nicked, really?" Roy said as he shrugged his shoulders. "It wasn't how can we help this fella whose actions saved scores of lives; it was just, I'm far too busy for your problems. Did you know that I got a two year banning order?"

Dave nodded.

"How does stuff like this happen?" Roy said before taking a sip of his piping hot coffee. "I reach out, desperate for help, and find myself arrested.

Dave remained quiet.

"So in answer to your question, how am I," Roy said before sitting down on the chair opposite Dave. "I'm racing towards the window every time I hear something outside and that is both day and night. I'm not using social media so I don't know how my family or friends are and I don't want ISIS tracking me to here and then turning up to finish the job."

Roy held up a basic Nokia phone.

"Do you believe that they have put you on their hit list?" Dave said.

"What kind of question is that?" Roy said as he placed his mug on the side table. "A police officer tells me I'm on the list because I foiled what they tried to do in the Black & Blue. Had I just run, along with everyone else, they could have injured or killed another thirty if not forty people. Do I think they want their revenge? Yes!"

"Roy," Dave said. "Are you sleeping?"

"I try to stay awake as long as possible so that I'm so damn tired that I don't dream," Roy said.

"Bad dreams?" Dave said.

"More like horrific, vivid, nightmares," Roy said as he reached for his coffee.

"Do you need something to help you sleep?" Dave said.

"No, what I need is something to stop the flashbacks and nightmares," Roy said as he rubbed his hands together.

"I'll make a note," Dave said.

"Great, I'm sure you making a note will get me straight off to sleep tonight without reliving it all over again," Roy thought.

"Do you know anything about the 'Prevent Programme'?" Dave said with a broad smile.

Roy shook his head

"It's a government led agency whose key role is to stop vulnerable individuals become terrorists," Dave said. "We work to support and protect people like you, Roy."

"Hold on, did you just say your job is stop people from becoming terrorists?" Roy said.

"Individuals, like you, who have encountered terrorism are considered vulnerable to radicalisation," Dave said as he put his hands on his knees.

"So you and the government have put me on a watch list?" Roy said.

"Yes, but it's not quite as bad as it sounds," Dave said awkwardly. "It's all part of the Government's counter-terrorism strategy."

"So, to be clear, you think because I didn't run away, like a number of uniformed police officers did, you now believe that I could be radicalised and what, carry out attacks on innocent people myself?" Roy said.

Dave nodded.

"It does happen."

"It gets worse, it just keeps on getting worse," Roy thought. *"When will this horrendous nightmare come to an end?"*

"There will be politically motivated, right wing extremists who will want to organise marches and the like in your name," Dave said. "It's important that you do not respond."

"All I want is help," Roy said. "Help to manage how I feel and to get all this behind me."

"Have any groups or individuals reached out to you?"

"No."

"Would you tell me if they did, Roy?" Dave said with his eyes firmly fixed on Roy.

"Yes."

"You must tell me if and when it happens," Dave said. "Will you do that?"

"I've just said yes," Roy said firmly.

"Good, so how are you settling here in Kent?" Dave said.

"It's quiet and the people are fine," Roy said. "A couple of people have recognised me and shook my hand, which was nice, but then I started over-thinking and imagined them telling friends who told more friends who went to the television people who then turned up en-masse with cameras and that's when ISIS make their move."

"Overthinking isn't healthy," Dave said.

"Tell me about it," Roy said bluntly. I've taken to walking the beach early in the morning before anyone else and keeping a very low profile."

"I never wanted any of this," Roy thought. *"I was born in London and I'm a Londoner through and through. This solitude is killing me."*

"I am here to help you to not get drawn into any kind of extremist ideology," Dave said with a curious smile. "I'm just a phone call away at any time.

"What is wrong with these people? I have no interest in extreme ideology," Roy thought. *"What I do need is help with these intrusive, distressing, thoughts. Removing these flashbacks and nightmares would be a great start along with this need to feel on high alert twenty four hours a day."*

"I'll be visiting you twice a week and will stay for ninety minutes," Dave said as he patted his knee.

"What if ISIS are plotting to take out my mum or Freya?" Roy thought.

"Yeah, okay," Roy replied.

"We can talk about all sorts of things," Dave said in a jovial tone. "I understand that you're an avid Millwall supporter."

"I am," Roy replied.

"What of it?" Roy thought.

"Well I'm a big Aston Villa supporter," Dave said as a broad smile swept across his face. "I'm a season ticket holder too."

"Okay," Roy said cautiously.

"So, we can talk about football, if you like."

"Well that would beat you telling me what is right and wrong because, Dave from Birmingham, I'm a forty seven year old man from Peckham and believe me, whilst growing up, my mum was very clear about right and wrong and the consequences for bad choices so I don't need you for that," Roy thought.

"Yeah, okay we can talk football," Roy said.

"I'm on an ISIS hit list and we can talk about football," Roy thought. *"I am struggling, really struggling to hold all this together."*

"To be honest, Roy, I shouldn't be doing this," Dave said gingerly. "You need professional help and a full assessment. You might be suffering with post-traumatic stress disorder for all I know and this Prevent Programme isn't going to help you resolve that."

There was a sudden noise outside and Roy was up and peering cautiously out through the curtains. It was a neighbour throwing a black plastic rubbish bag into a bin.

"Are you okay, Roy?" Dave said as he quickly got to his feet.

"Yeah, it was nothing," Roy said as he let go of the curtain.

"I hope Tracy and Freya are okay," Roy thought. *"Things got a little heated the last time we spoke on the phone."*

"You don't seem to be here," Dave said with a quizzical expression.

"I'm fine," Roy said.

"I must try and stop these negative thoughts from just invading my head," Roy thought as he walked Dave the short distance to the front door.

"I'll be back in a couple of days," Dave said as he shook Roy's hand and stepped out into the caravan park.

"Have a safe trip back," Roy said before glancing to his left then right before closing the door and locking it.

Roy decided to change his routine and started walking the beach just before dark so he could try and wear himself out to the point where he could relax and have a dreamless sleep. It didn't help. The relationship with Tracy and Freya broke down as the lack of sleep, mounting stress and unresolved trauma affected Roy's judgement and behaviour.

Dave visited twice a week. On one occasion Roy had peered out of his curtain to see the Prevent councillor talking with neighbours and park staff before pointing at Roy's caravan which added significantly to his paranoia.

Roy would spend his days and nights traipsing aimlessly around his caravan, looking out the window at every noise and creating multiple scenarios in his mind where ISIS were spying on him and just waiting patiently for the right opportunity to finish the job they started back in Borough Market.

The solitude was taking its toll with anger, minor fits of rage and irritability.

Whilst Roy looked forward to his appointments at London's St Thomas and Guys Hospital the initial excitement would fade and be replaced by dread, paranoia and anxiety as the Mosque sang out the call to prayer. His mind would create a hundred and one incredibly violent scenarios where he would be chased by hundreds of raging terrorists thirsting for the blood of Roy Larner.

The nurses were wonderful, attentive and for a short time removed the dark cloud that was never far away.

Roy dreaded the return train ride back to New Romney and his self-imposed prison.

Chapter 28

June 3rd 2018

It was the first anniversary of the terror attack on London Bridge. Roy travelled up on the train to attend the ceremony at Southwark Cathedral for those who died and were injured. The Prime Minister, Theresa May, Labour leader, Jeremy Corbyn; the Mayor of London, Sadiq Khan; the Home Secretary, Sajid Javid, Diane Abbott; the Duke and Duchess of Gloucester and members of the emergency services laid wreaths and floral tributes.

Two men in dark suits approached Roy.

"Roy Larner?"

Roy nodded.

"I will only tell you this once," whispered the close protection officer. "Do not, under any circumstances, attempt to speak with any members of parliament."

"I just want to ask for help," Roy said.

"Consider yourself told," the second close protection officer muttered.

"No one is listening, no one is helping," Roy thought. *"I just want someone, anyone to get me the help I need. How much longer must this nightmare go on?"*

The Bishop of Southwark addressed the service with a message of hope and faith and touched on the seeds of hope being sown as those who stood their ground and refused to let terror triumph.

"I stood my ground," Roy thought. *"What good has it done me? I'm on a terrorist's watch list and live alone at the far end of Kent with no friends and no one to really talk to. I sit here and watch these public figures go through a planned out routine while being photographed for the newspapers and filmed for television. It's all fake and good publicity. They don't truly care."*

Eight candles were lit during the service, one for each of those murdered by the terrorists.

Christine Archibald
James McMullen
Sebastien Belanger
Xaviar Thomas
Alexandre Pigeard
Kirsty Boden
Zara Zelenak
Ignacio Echeverria

The Prime Minister, Theresa May, paid tribute to those who died and the many who were injured. She praised the bravery of the emergency services and those who intervened or came to the aid of others. She described the attack as a cowardly attempt to strike at the heart of our freedoms and concluded that the resolve to stand firm and overcome the threat together has never been stronger.

The Mayor of London, Sadiq Khan, spoke of the terror attacks at Westminster, London Bridge, Finsbury Park and Parsons Green and how proud he was of the way London responded by standing united in staying true to our values and way of life.

Roy watched as the dignitaries shook hands with police officers in front of the live television cameras

"Maybe," Roy thought as the service came to an end, *"the Mayor will spot me and say a few words. I could ask him for help. He's the Mayor of London, he could help me."*

Security lined the pathway to the exit. Roy called out to the Mayor to turn. He would have gladly settled for an acknowledgement with a simple handshake or smile but Sadiq Khan ignored Roy and left the cathedral and sped away in one of the waiting cars.

The outside of the cathedral was packed with members of the public paying their respects. With both the close protection officers gone, Roy left the building. As he stepped out onto the pavement he was instantly recognised and scores of men, woman and children lined up to thank him and shake his hand. Roy was feeling overwhelmed.

One elderly gentleman stood a few feet away. He was holding the hand of what Roy believed to be his eight- maybe ten-year old grandson.

"Hello," Roy said with a warm, friendly, smile.

The elderly man approached him and held out his working class hand.

Roy shook it warmly.

"Here you go Roy," the elderly man said as Roy felt something against his palm. "Get yourself a drink.

"Thank you," Roy said without looking down at the note.

Roy watched as the elderly man held his grandson's hand tightly and followed the green cross code before crossing the road.

Roy looked down at the note.

"What?" Roy thought. *"This is fifty pounds!"*

Roy was instantly touched, choked up and brought to tears.

"He was an everyday working class guy and fifty pounds is a lot of money," Roy thought as he walked back towards Borough Market. *"The sentiment means so much more than the money. Thank you, thank you from the very bottom of my heart!"*

The words 'London United' were projected onto the bridge while Roy took the last train to Folkestone. As each mile passed away from his home, London, he could feel the dread, anxiety and paranoia return.

***

Roy was stunned to find that there wasn't a single taxi outside the station to take him the fourteen miles along the coast road to New Romney. The roads were empty, but the summer air was warm so he started walking. It was well after 4.00am before Roy arrived back at the caravan park, shattered. He slipped off his shoes, got undressed and fell onto the bed. Within seconds he had fallen into his first deep dreamless sleep in months.

Chapter 29

Dave Allport continued to visit twice each week. He would always ask if any right-wing terror groups had reached out to Roy before engaging in football chat.

Increasingly, as Roy sat alone in his caravan, he felt a persistent feeling of sadness in addition to the paranoia and anxiety. When he wasn't imagining being viciously attacked by screaming, machete wielding terrorists, he thought about London, Millwall, his mum, Freya, his friends and the life he had before the London Bridge terror attack. Roy was sinking into a depressive state with thoughts of suicide and ending it all trying to push their way to the front of his mind as a solution to his overwhelming feelings of hopelessness.

To avoid sleeping and the nightly nightmares Roy, while in London, had bought one hundred pounds worth of the illegal slimming drug amphetamine. He took just enough to keep him awake throughout the night and then as the effects wore off, he would fall into a dreamless sleep the next morning.

Roy sat on the sofa as the sun went down.

"I'm done with this," Roy thought as a minor rage surged through his body. *"I miss my mum, Freya and my life in London. This isn't fair, none of this is fair!"*

A surge of anger, rage and frustration raced from the pit of his stomach to his head and hands in a microsecond. Roy leapt up from the sofa.

"Arghhh!" Roy yelled out at the top of his voice. "I've had enough!"

Roy grabbed an empty coffee cup.

"No more!" Roy cried out before throwing the cup at the flat screen television.

SMASH!

As the crashing sound rang in his ears he bounded over and kicked the screen.

"No, no, no!" he bellowed, kicking the broken television across the floor.

"Come on then, take me if you want!" Roy shrieked before grabbing the side table by the leg and hurling it towards the window.

SMASH!

"I'm here, come on then," Roy yelled, holding his hands up and motioning the ice cold outside world in. "I'm done with hiding!"

The rage continued to race around his body while he paced around the caravan.

Several minutes later and the rage simmered. Roy slumped back onto the chair and looked out of the broken window at the night sky.

"I can't do this anymore," Roy thought as he clenched and unclenched his fists. *"I will not cower or hide from anyone anywhere, tooled up or not. Nobody will stop me living out my life in the way I choose to live."*

Roy's eyes were drawn down from the sky to the blue flashing lights that were now lighting up the inside of his caravan.

Knock, knock!

"Police, open up!"

Roy unclenched his fists and took a shot from his inhaler before opening the door.

The two officers stepped into the caravan. Roy immediately recognised one as an officer that had knocked on the caravan door and introduced himself. He told Roy that the Prevent Organisation had been in touch. Roy took it that he was now being spied on like he really was a terrorist. Roy had told the officer that he needed help and that no one was listening.

The second officer looked around the caravan while the first officer engaged Roy in casual conversation about what had happened to the caravan. Once the officer found Roy's small amount of amphetamine, Roy was arrested.

"You're kidding me," Roy protested. "It's less than a hundred pounds worth and I use it to avoid sleep and the nightmares."

Roy was bundled into the back of the police car and then driven to Folkestone Police Station where he was processed and held in a cell overnight. The following morning he was brought before a magistrate and then shipped off in a prison van to HMP Swaleside , a category 'B' prison, on the Isle of Sheppey.

"I just don't believe that this is all happening to me," Roy thought as he was led onto the wing. *"Piers Morgan and the press tell me that I'm a hero and the government have just left me to struggle."*

More than half the prisoners at HMP Swaleside are serving life sentences. The ethnic prison population is between 30% - 40% and there are acute staff shortfalls and high levels of violence.

Roy was to share a cell with two other inmates. One who called himself 'Goose' and was a former Hells Angel on remand for a domestic dispute. The second inmate was Roger, a young man in his early thirties who had been caught fiddling his employer's books to fund a blossoming romance.

The three men agreed that they would share what little they had, which created a sustainable bond when locked away in a cell for most of the day. Goose would relay stories of riding around London with his biker mates and the occasional tear ups with other clubs. His partner, Shaz, had convinced Goose to allow a third person to join their relationship for adventure and to explore their sexuality. He had believed that they were secure in their relationship and having watched adult movies online with Shaz, he agreed to the threesome with Trevor, a young lad who worked with Shaz. Goose told them that it had indeed been adventurous and exciting and had taken their relationship to another level. However, when he returned from work earlier than expected and found Shaz in bed with Trevor, he was furious. Trevor had bolted for the door leaving most of his clothes in a pile on the bedroom floor. An argument ensued with Goose telling her to pack her things and to get out. Shaz called the police and fabricated a story about threats with his licensed shotgun that had him arrested and jailed without bail.

Roger told his cellmates that he never been particularly successful with girls but had met a stunningly beautiful girl called Chloe while out in London with friends from work. Chloe had chatted with Roger at the bar. However, having had a few too many, he over exaggerated his wealth and position. Roger had been stunned when Chloe agreed to meet him again. Working in the finance department had given Roger access to moving funds by paying suppliers and receiving payments from customers. Roger had hired a Porsche 911 to meet with Chloe for dinner at The Tower Hotel by Tower Bridge. He discovered that Chloe came from money and a family that developed properties all over the capital. Fearing that he would lose her, he created a plan to embezzle the company's money by creating fake invoices and purchase orders. At first it had just been a few thousand pounds to finance the hired sports car and nights out. Roger concluded that to keep Chloe he had to reinvent himself and began to increase the number of invoices with a growing number of fake suppliers. It allowed him to rent a penthouse apartment in the smartest part of town and fund a wardrobe fit to be seen in with Chloe at VIP clubs in the West End. While away on a short break to New York with Chloe, the auditors arrived and discovered the gaping great holes in the books and called in the police.

Roy explained that he was there because the police had found one hundred pounds worth of amphetamine at his home.

Outside of prison some of the newspapers had overly exaggerated the amount of 'speed' involved and had insinuated that Roy, the Lion of London Bridge, was a drug dealer.

The two weeks at HMP Swaleside passed slowly and finally Roy was taken to Canterbury Court where he explained that he had been suffering with PTSD and insomnia and that the small amount of drugs found by the police were for his own personal use in a desperate attempt to avoid sleep and the nightmares. Roy pleaded guilty to possession and the charges for dealing were dropped. He was given a three month suspended sentence.

Roy returned to his caravan in New Romney only to find his name plastered all over the newspapers and members of the press knocking on his neighbours' doors in a vain hope of finding a story.

"I can't do this any longer," Roy thought as he peered out of his caravan window at what appeared to be a reporter knocking on the door of the caravan opposite. *"I've got just two choices. I can end it all right here and now or just accept that help isn't coming now or ever and I need to just grow a pair and take back control of my life."*

"I'm going back to London, to my home, my family and my friends!" Roy said defiantly.

Roy took a shot from his inhaler and began to pack up a few personal belongings.

"I'm done with hiding," Roy thought as he pushed a couple of Polo shirts into his bag. *"I'll face anything and anyone who stands between me and getting my life back!"*

Roy locked the caravan door and scowled at the newspaper reporter who looked as if he were about to ask him a question.

"With the exception of The Sun you have all mugged me off in one way or another," Roy thought as he stared down at the reporter. *"I took on three Islamic murderers and saved people's lives! What have you lot ever done!"*

Roy took a private taxi to Folkestone. He stared out of the window as the driver passed through Dymchurch, Sandgate and Hythe.

"I will not miss you," Roy thought as the sea came into view. *"I was born and grew up in the greatest city in the world and now I'm going home."*

Chapter 30

"Roy! Come in, come in," Phyllis said, throwing her arms around her son.

The embrace had felt strange and almost alien as Roy had no memories of being hugged before, it just wasn't something that happened in the Larner home.

Phyllis ushered Roy in and closed the front door.

"I know exactly what you need," Phyllis said as she motioned Roy to go into the living room while she went into the kitchen. "A nice cup of tea."

"That would be great Mum," Roy said as he looked at the familiar surroundings of his family home.

Roy sat on the settee and smiled warmly as Phyllis brought in two steaming hot cups of strong tea.

"There you go," Phyllis said with a broad smile. "It's just as you like it."

"Thanks Mum," Roy said as he blew the steam away and took a small sip. "It's perfect."

Roy told Phyllis about his struggles in New Romney and the lack of professional help. He took the opportunity to tell the true story behind the one hundred pounds worth of 'speed' and why he took it. Phyllis wasn't surprised that some of the newspapers had exaggerated the facts and made out that Roy was some kind of king pin drug dealer.

"They will say anything to sell newspapers," Phyllis said.

Roy explained that he could no longer bear the solitude and self-imposed prison sentence he had given himself by moving out of London to the far ends of Kent.

"I just needed help, Mum," Roy said as he put both hands on his knees. "But instead they put me on the terrorist watch list."

Phyllis shook head and a single tear streamed down her cheek.

"I didn't realise it was that bad, son."

Roy told her about the anxiety and raging paranoia which was fuelled by being alone with just the horrific memories to taunt and haunt him every day.

"I had to leave it behind and try to take control of my life again," Roy said.

"Well you did the right thing by coming back home, son," Phyllis said. "Now drink your tea before it gets cold."

Roy was to stay in the bedroom he had as a teenager.

Later that day there was a knock at the door.

"I told Costas you were back home," Phyllis said before opening the front door.

Costas bounded down the hallway with a huge grin and shook Roy warmly by the hand.

"It's damn good to see you Roy," Costas said.

Roy retold his story while Phyllis made more tea.

"There is a reason why there are so very few true heroes in the world," Costas said as he sat down opposite Roy. "Don't get me wrong, with so much poverty, famine and violence in the world, we need heroes now more than ever."

Roy nodded his head.

"You have always been so good to me," Roy thought as he listened intently.

"The kind of heroic behaviour you displayed at Borough Market isn't normal, Roy," Costas said as he leant forward and held Roy's gaze. "What you did was far from conventional and that scares people, particularly those in power with influence, because heroes are not ordinary, they are extraordinary."

"It just happened," Roy said. "I couldn't run and needed to fight back especially having seen and read about what happened in Manchester and on Westminster Bridge."

"Ninety percent of people disseminate responsibility in difficult, life threatening situations, and just expect somebody else, anyone else, to become the hero and save the day," Costas said before thanking Phyllis for the cup of tea.

Images of young men trampling over women and children to escape the knife wielding Jihadis filled his mind.

Roy nodded as he remembered seeing uniformed police officers racing away from the armed murderers.

"It's about moral courage and most people just don't have it," Costas said as he shook his head. "They see no wrong in failing to help others in need."

"Believe me Costas, I'm not sure why I did it some days," Roy thought.

"When it all kicked off at Borough Market your primeval instincts kicked in, Roy, and without any consideration for your own safety you put your life at risk to help others. There was no long drawn out thought process, you just acted immediately and lives were saved," Costas said. "I'm proud of you Roy, but the sad reality is that incredible acts of heroism are rarely rewarded by society. In my personal opinion I believe that you should have run, like everyone else, and just looked out for yourself."

"I couldn't do that," Roy said firmly.

"I know, and from what you've been telling, me I truly cannot understand why anyone would put their life on the line," Costas said, slowly shaking his head.

The rest of the evening passed pleasantly with Costas telling Roy about his work and Arsenal Football Club. Roy, for the first time in months, felt at peace and was happy to just be in the company of his mother and Costas.

The following morning, over breakfast, Roy decided that he should phone the 'Prevent Programme' and tell them that he was longer in New Romney but was staying with his mum on the Ledbury Estate in Peckham. The woman was friendly enough and said that she would pass on the information.

Four days later a van load of uniformed police officers arrived on the estate. They set about bashing loudly on the front door and yelling out to open up. Phyllis, still in her nightwear, opened the door and the officers rushed into the flat, almost knocking her to the floor. Roy had been sleeping better than he had in months and was still in bed.

"Larner, get out of that pit!" an officer said as he stood over Roy's bed.

"What's going on?" Roy said as he looked up at the six police officers standing around his bed.

"You're nicked, son!" the lead officer said, making a grab for Roy's arm.

"I don't understand," Roy said as he tried to put the trousers an officer had just flung at him on. "What am I supposed to have done?"

"You're in breach, matey, and you shouldn't be here," the officer said, motioning Roy to hurry up and get dressed.

"My mum is eighty years old and I still need to see her," Roy pleaded.

"What's going on," Phyllis said. "Why are you doing this to my son?"

"Move along, this is police business," a second officer said while moving towards Phyllis.

"Don't you touch her," Roy warned.

"Just get a move on Larner," the lead officer said with a sneer. "We haven't had our breakfast yet!"

"This is crazy," Roy thought as he did up his shirt buttons. *"What the hell am I supposed to have done?"*

Roy was handcuffed and then frog marched out of his bedroom and down the hallway.

Phyllis was visibly distressed as she stood by the kitchen door watching the hoard of uniformed police officers manhandle her son.

"Why the hell are you doing this?" Roy yelled out. "I've saved people's lives!"

"Shut it Larner," the officer hissed through gritted teeth. "You're nicked, so shut it and move!"

Roy was bundled into the back of the police van and was surrounded by unsmiling officers until they arrived at the police station where he was processed and placed in a holding cell. Roy used his customary phone call to contact his solicitor.

The solicitor arrived within the hour and immediately took control of the situation. Roy explained that police officers had treated him like some kind of criminal and caused huge stress on his elderly mother. It transpired that the 'Prevent Organisation' had pushed for Roy's arrest, claiming that he shouldn't be at his mother's home. They had also contacted the DVLC and advised them that Roy Larner had an alcohol dependency problem. They immediately removed Roy's driving licence for thirty six months. Roy explained that he didn't have a problem and only drank socially when he was out and never at home. There was no appeal process and based on the report received by the 'Prevent Programme' the three year driving ban remained in place.

"This is crazy," Roy thought as he paced around the interview room. *"I could have been arrested and prosecuted for drinking and driving and only received a twelve month ban. I'm innocent, so why the hell are they doing this to me?"*

Roy made a formal complaint, through his solicitor, about the way he had been manhandled by the uniformed police officers, but it was met with a unified brick wall. The official response was deny-deny-deny, and that everything was done by the book.

Roy was released and he returned to his mother's home on the Ledbury Estate. She was visibly shaken and for the first time Roy acknowledged just how old his mother was. Costas, as ever, was supportive, and asked if he had applied for criminal damages compensation and if not he should do because it had to be done within two years.

Roy made the application.

The Criminal Injuries Scheme is government funded and was created to compensate victims of serious crime in Great Britain. Whilst the scheme acknowledges that no amount of compensation could make up for the harm and suffering caused to the victims of serious crime, it was an acknowledgement of the harm done and an important gesture of public sympathy.

Roy was denied compensation despite damaging his arm and being repeatedly stabbed and slashed. The inquest was shown footage of Roy being savagely stabbed in the stomach and advised that Roy spent twelve days in hospital where he received eighty stitches to his head, ear, neck, arms and hands.

The authority rules dictate that victims of a crime cannot claim if they have criminal convictions.

Roy was gutted by the decision and told the Sun newspaper that the money would have helped him to re-build his life.

It was yet another knock for Roy but he was determined to stay in London and put the horrors and systematic let downs behind him. Tracy Johnson, a friend, made a point of seeking Roy out and told him straight that enough was enough and that he was to come home with her. The flat was tiny and cramped, but words could not describe just how appreciative Roy was. Tracy's daughter had just given birth to a son so the family home was full of love and happiness with the new arrival. Roy had never experienced such personal kindness in his life and was grateful to be able to go to bed at 9.00pm and sleep soundly until the next day. Tracy provided more care and help in a week than he had received from the authorities in years.

Tracy and Roy became partners.

Tracy continues to provide overwhelming care, love and support and is the primary reason that Roy is making such good, solid progress.

Epilogue

It's 2022 and five years since the terror attack on London Bridge and I'm in a place now where I can safely reflect on the past horrors. The encouraging messages of support from football fans and clubs from all over the UK has been tremendous. I think I've learnt that whilst the passion for our team may divide us, on match day the love we have for football unites us all.

It would be wrong for me to say that every public figure I came into contact with was little more than a public relations exercise with a fake handshake for the camera, although at times it certainly felt that way. By stark contrast, the handshakes and greetings from the real people of every race, colour and creed have been genuine, warm and most gratefully received.

The divide between those that govern us and the public has never been farther apart in my lifetime. I watch how politicians never answer a direct yes or no question on television before swiftly turning the topic to a political point that they want to make before the interviewer runs out of time and has to move on. I suppose I'm waking up to the illusion created by those who wish to maintain control of the masses.

In 2020 MI5 acknowledged an alarming 43,000 people posed a potential terrorist threat. I struggle to understand why the government, any government, isn't taking preventative measures by pro-actively removing the threat and protecting the innocent lives of those they serve.

I don't want to accept that terror attacks are to be accepted as part and parcel of living in a major city. If, however, I am forced to accept that is the case, then surely there should be an effective aftercare system for those of us who survive.

On a personal note, I decided, in the end, to dig deep, take control and help myself. I remember Costas, my dad, saying that life is a journey and happiness isn't a destination and that life can be messy, but with time, it all comes right in the end. I was extremely fortunate in finding positive encouragement from my friends, my football club, Millwall, and the fabulous British public. I'm taking one day at a time. My arms are still weak but I am healing slowly and there are more good days now than bad. There are times when I struggle to understand how I could be left to suffer and why more help wasn't given. I still have this vivid memory, while in New Romney, of a Millwall mate phoning and inviting me up to the Sunderland game. It was just what I needed to hear because the self-imposed solitude was really taking its toll. It was to be an early start as I needed to be in London by 6.00am so I hired a car. After a single cup of coffee I set off. It was just after 4.00am. The roads were empty and I made great progress until I reached the M2. I was travelling at 70mph along the inside lane of the motorway when I spotted a set of blue lights racing up behind me in the rear view mirror. The flashing lights acted like a trigger, and they still do. I felt a horrendous tidal wave of fear and anxiety wash over me as memories of the terror attack in 2017 came rushing back into my mind. With the police car now on my tail I indicated and pulled over onto the hard shoulder. I wound down my window and took several deep breaths of the fresh, cold, morning air. The young officer bounded over and said 'Roy Larner'. I nodded in a state of shock and confusion. How did he know my name? Are the authorities spying on me and why? The officer asked for my documents before sending me on my way. I can't help but wonder why they, whoever they are, couldn't have put the same kind of effort into helping me cope with the trauma following the terror attack as they did to keep an eye on my movements.

On a totally separate note I simply must add that I'm extremely proud of my daughter, Freya, who plans to go to University and then train to become a nurse.

My sincere hope is that those with power will re-look at my criminal injury compensation claim and do the 'British' thing which is to be fair and reasonable in all things.

Knowing all that I now know, I ask myself occasionally: Would I do it again?

What do you think?

Roy Larner aka The Lion of London Bridge.

The Lion of London Bridge

A poem by Kelso Simon (Poet & Author)

The Lion of London Bridge

Do you know what he did?

He looked death in the face and fought and saved, that's the Lion of London Bridge

An ordinary bloke

Done an extraordinary thing

But the powers that be would rather you forget, but his name we all should sing

The scars are there to see

Because he did not flee

He fought for the people on that day,

Black or white, he or she

They tried to bring him down and drag his name through the dirt

So they ignore his pain and they ignore his hurt

But me I won't forget, and to Roy I must salute

It doesn't matter how they try to bring his name into dispute

If you were in his shoes what would you have done?

Would you have stayed and fought,

Or would you have chose to run?

Because I will tell you this, and I will say it plain

Most of us would have ran and let them bastards state their claim

But Roy he chose to fight, and let them think again

So don't not forget his agony, and don't forget his pain

No matter who you are, from a Gooner to a Yid

Remember the name Roy Larner, remember what he did.

What About Roy Larner?

Two years ago today three Muslim terrorists murdered eight and injured a further 48 in attacks at London Bridge and Borough Market. During the fortnight inquiry into the attack, there has been one name that has been glossed over, a man whose actions have been routinely erased by the powers that be. He was pointedly not invited to the anniversary of the attack, his name not mentioned, and he was knowingly left off the honour call, whilst the deputy commissioner, Sir Craig Mackey, was polishing his boots to collect a gallantry medal for locking his car doors and radioing for help during the Westminster Bridge attack, Roy Larner was busily being forgotten. For the powers that be he is just the wrong sort of hero.

Four or five beers down, drinking with a mate in the Black and Blue in Borough Market, Roy Larner was enjoying an evening pint, unaware that a path of destruction was headed straight to his table. Having already murdered eight people, the three attackers burst into the bar and set about the patrons, one of them headed straight for Roy Larner. With ceramic knives strapped to his hands he screamed "This is for Allah". "Fuck you, I'm Millwall" Roy replied and a hero of the people was born. Stabbed twice in the stomach in quick succession Mr Larner fought on and remained boxing, offering enough resistance that one of the attackers came back to assist his fellow Jihadi who was grappling with Roy. The attackers concentrated on him and another drinker, disrupting the planned path to the contained diners in the restaurant and the other drinkers. The terrorists left the Black and Blue and were then shot dead. Having been stabbed and slashed nine times Roy Larner was rushed to hospital.

Over the next couple of days the media championed Roy's courage and immense bravery. After being discharged from hospital he appeared on Good Morning Britain and Fox News, modestly retelling the events of that fateful evening. Then the unthinkable happened, the logic of which is so impossible to follow that it is difficult to comprehend. Aspects of the media went looking for dirt on him. The Independent and the Socialist Worker ran stories about run-ins he had with people, an altercation he had had with a member of the public. The morality of the press has always been absent, but to look for dirt and try and disparage the actions of a citizen who stopped three murderers slaughtering restaurant goers is one of the most revolting things I have ever heard. We used to put up statues and write songs about brave men who carried out brave actions, now we ruin them.

You wouldn't have to dig very far to find dirt on anyone. Why does a man who just wanted to have a beer have to be subjected to a character check?

Does a hero have to be a saint? Does a civilian having a quiet drink who's unfortunate enough to find himself within a terrorist atrocity have to be an unblemished character? If you fell on a train track would you want the man who rescued you to have a completely uncheckered past? Why do we let editors who knowingly print fake photos of abuse putting innocent soldiers lives at risk, decide on what is right and what is wrong? Why do we let industries who hack phones of murdered teenagers become the moral gatekeepers?

***

During the World Cup after the England Panama game, Nice Threads, Mate ran into Roy Larner at Elephant. We stood and chatted for about half an hour, a nice down to earth Londoner. Hearing how badly he has been let down made me think of soldiering, how you can be used and dumped. How you can be used for your assets but your lot won't change, you can play their game but you will suffer, you will give your all when it is required and the same obstacles will be put in your way. Roy Larner was a hero who never asked to be put in the situation he was put in, they used him for his aggression and force when they wanted it, they used his actions to sell papers, they used his story to sell advertising revenue, they used his "Fuck you, I'm Millwall" to sell merchandise and they used one moment of his past to destroy him. To all those people who built him up and tore him down to make a few quid, realise this is a man's life you are dealing with. Used and dumped seems to be the history of men like Mr Larner for hundreds of years in this country. He would be the first to say he is not perfect but they didn't care about perfection when he was the obstacle that stopped terrorists slaying punters in the Black and Blue. "For once in my life I did the right thing," Roy said to me "And look how you got treated," I replied. Seeing his scars is a very sobering experience and those who have attempted to break him should be made to see them.

So here you are Roy, here is the George Cross they refuse to give you. Good luck mate, you're a hero to the people. Some are honoured by elites and others are honoured by the people. Those who gave knighthoods to Jimmy Saville and Cyril Smith think you're not their type of hero... Roy Larner GC, the Lion of London Bridge, fear no foe.

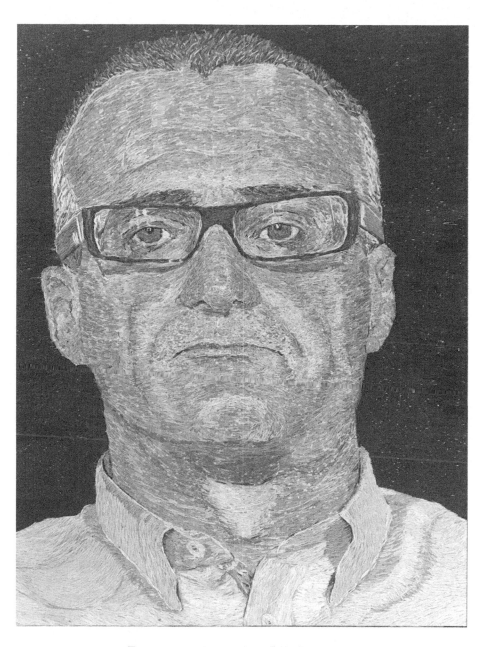

Roy up-close by Bill Borrett

Roy by Bill Borrett

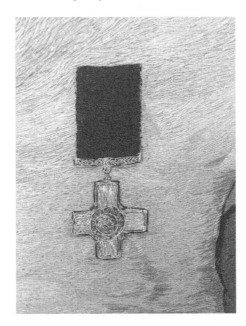

The George Cross by Bill Borrett

Books with Dean Rinaldi

Alfie Kray The Asset by S Clark Kray

Villain No Remorse by Al McIntosh

Villain No Remorse II by Al McIntosh

Villain No Remorse III by Al McIntosh

King of the Teds: Inception by Dave Bartram

King of the Teds: Unification by Dave Bartram

King of the Teds: Infiltration by Dave Bartram

Walking with an open Heart by Dusty White

The Machiavellian by R A Griffiths

The S.A.D Road to Happiness by Alison Parker

Facebook: Dean Rinaldi Ghostwriter Publisher & Mentor

Website: www.deanrinaldi-ghostwriter.com

Made in United States
North Haven, CT
20 December 2022

29339578R00174